The Uninhabited House

By Charlotte Riddell

First published in 1875

CONTENTS

MISS BLAKE—FROM MEMORY

If ever a residence, "suitable in every respect for a family of position," haunted a lawyer's offices, the "Uninhabited House," about which I have a story to tell, haunted those of Messrs. Craven and Son, No. 200, Buckingham Street, Strand.

It did not matter in the least whether it happened to be let or unlet: in either case, it never allowed Mr. Craven or his clerks, of whom I was one, to forget its existence.

When let, we were in perpetual hot water with the tenant; when unlet, we had to endeavour to find some tenant to take that unlucky house.

Happy were we when we could get an agreement signed for a couple of years—although we always had misgivings that the war waged with the last occupant would probably have to be renewed with his successor.

Still, when we were able to let the desirable residence to a solvent individual, even for twelve months, Mr. Craven rejoiced.

He knew how to proceed with the tenants who came blustering, or threatening, or complaining, or bemoaning; but he did not know what to do with Miss Blake and her letters, when no person was liable for the rent.

All lawyers—I am one myself, and can speak from a long and varied experience—all lawyers, even the very hardest, have one client, at all events, towards whom they exhibit much forbearance, for whom they feel a certain sympathy, and in whose interests they take a vast deal of trouble for very little pecuniary profit.

A client of this kind favours me with his business—he has favoured me with it for many years past. Each first of January I register a vow he shall cost me no more time or money. On each last day of December I find he is deeper in my debt than he was on the same date a twelvemonth previous.

I often wonder how this is—why we, so fierce to one human being, possibly honest and well-meaning enough, should be as wax in the hand of the moulder, when another individual, perhaps utterly disreputable, refuses to take "No" for an answer.

Do we purchase our indulgences in this way? Do we square our accounts with our own consciences by remembering that, if we have been as stone to Dick, Tom, and Harry, we have melted at the first appeal of Jack?

My principal, Mr. Craven—than whom a better man never breathed—had an unprofitable client, for whom he entertained feelings of the profoundest pity, whom he treated with a rare courtesy. That lady was Miss Blake; and when the old house on the Thames stood tenantless, Mr. Craven's bed did not prove one of roses.

In our firm there was no son—Mr. Craven had been the son; but the old father was dead, and our chief's wife had brought him only daughters.

Still the title of the firm remained the same, and Mr. Craven's own signature also.

He had been junior for such a number of years, that, when Death sent a royal invitation to his senior, he was so accustomed to the old form, that he, and all in his employment, tacitly agreed it was only fitting he should remain junior to the end.

A good man. I, of all human beings, have reason to speak well of him. Even putting the undoubted fact of all lawyers keeping one unprofitable client into the scales, if he had not been very good he must have washed his hands of Miss Blake and her niece's house long before the period at which this story opens.

The house did not belong to Miss Blake. It was the property of her niece, a certain Miss Helena Elmsdale, of whom Mr. Craven always spoke as that "poor child."

She was not of age, and Miss Blake managed her few pecuniary affairs.

Besides the "desirable residence, suitable," etcetera, aunt and niece had property producing about sixty-five pounds a year. When we could let the desirable residence, handsomely furnished, and with every convenience that could be named in the space of a half-guinea advertisement, to a family from the country, or an officer just returned from India, or to an invalid who desired a beautiful and quiet abode within an easy drive of the West End—when we could do this, I say, the income of aunt and niece rose to two hundred and sixty-five pounds a year, which made a very material difference to Miss Blake.

4

When we could not let the house, or when the payment of the rent was in dispute, Mr. Craven advanced the lady various five and ten pound notes, which, it is to be hoped, were entered duly to his credit in the Eternal Books. In the mundane records kept in our offices, they always appeared as debits to William Craven's private account.

As for the young men about our establishment, of whom I was one, we anathematised that house. I do not intend to reproduce the language we used concerning it at one period of our experience, because eventually the evil wore itself out, as most evils do, and at last we came to look upon the desirable residence as an institution of our firm—as a sort of cause célèbre, with which it was creditable to be associated—as a species of remarkable criminal always on its trial, and always certain to be defended by Messrs. Craven and Son.

In fact, the Uninhabited House—for uninhabited it usually was, whether anyone was answerable for the rent or not—finally became an object of as keen interest to all Mr. Craven's clerks as it became a source of annoyance to him.

So the beam goes up and down. While Mr. Craven pooh-poohed the complaints of tenants, and laughed at the idea of a man being afraid of a ghost, we did not laugh, but swore. When, however, Mr. Craven began to look serious about the matter, and hoped some evil-disposed persons were not trying to keep the place tenantless, our interest in the old house became absorbing. And as our interest in the residence grew, so, likewise, did our appreciation of Miss Blake.

We missed her when she went abroad—which she always did the day a fresh agreement was signed—and we welcomed her return to England and our offices with effusion. Safely I can say no millionaire ever received such an ovation as fell to the lot of Miss Blake when, after a foreign tour, she returned to those lodgings near Brunswick Square, which her residence ought, I think, to have rendered classic.

She never lost an hour in coming to us. With the dust of travel upon her, with the heat and burden of quarrels with railway porters, and encounters with cabmen, visible to anyone who chose to read the signs of

5

the times, Miss Blake came pounding up our stairs, wanting to see Mr. Craven.

If that gentleman was engaged, she would sit down in the general office, and relate her latest grievance to a posse of sympathising clerks.

"And he says he won't pay the rent," was always the refrain of these lamentations.

"It is in Ireland he thinks he is, poor soul!" she was wont to declare.

"We'll teach him different, Miss Blake," the spokesman of the party would declare; whilst another ostentatiously mended a pen, and a third brought down a ream of foolscap and laid it with a thump before him on the desk.

"And, indeed, you're all decent lads, though full of your tricks," Miss Blake would sometimes remark, in a tone of gentle reproof. "But if you had a niece just dying with grief, and a house nobody will live in on your hands, you would not have as much heart for fun, I can tell you that."

Hearing which, the young rascals tried to look sorrowful, and failed.

In the way of my profession I have met with many singular persons, but I can safely declare I never met with any person so singular as Miss Blake.

She was—I speak of her in the past tense, not because she is dead, but because times and circumstances have changed since the period when we both had to do with the Uninhabited House, and she has altered in consequence—one of the most original people who ever crossed my path.

Born in the north of Ireland, the child of a Scottish-Ulster mother and a Connaught father, she had ingeniously contrived to combine in her own person the vices of two distinct races, and exclude the virtues of both.

Her accent was the most fearful which could be imagined. She had the brogue of the West grafted on the accent of the North. And yet there was a variety about her even in this respect. One never could tell, from visit to visit, whether she proposed to pronounce "written" as "wrutten" or "wretten";[Footnote: The wife of a celebrated Indian officer stated that she once, in the north of Ireland, heard Job's utterance thus rendered—"Oh! that my words were wrutten, that they were prented in a buke."] whether she

6

would elect to style her parents, to whom she made frequent reference, her "pawpaw and mawmaw," or her "pepai and memai."

It all depended with whom Miss Blake had lately been most intimate. If she had been "hand and glove" with a "nob" from her own country—she was in no way reticent about thus styling her grander acquaintances, only she wrote the word "knob"—who thought to conceal his nationality by "awing" and "hawing," she spoke about people being "morried" and wearing "sockcloth and oshes." If, on the contrary, she had been thrown into the society of a lady who so far honoured England as to talk as some people do in England, we had every A turned into E, and every U into O, while she minced her words as if she had been saying "niminy piminy" since she first began to talk, and honestly believed no human being could ever have told she had been born west of St. George's Channel.

But not merely in accent did Miss Blake evidence the fact that her birth had been the result of an injudicious cross; the more one knew of her, the more clearly one saw the wrong points she threw out.

Extravagant to a fault, like her Connaught father, she was in no respect generous, either from impulse or calculation.

Mean about minor details, a turn of character probably inherited from the Ulster mother, she was utterly destitute of that careful and honest economy which is an admirable trait in the natives of the north of Ireland, and which enables them so frequently, after being strictly just, to be much more than liberal.

Honest, Miss Blake was not—or, for that matter, honourable either. Her indebtedness to our firm could not be considered other than a matter of honour, and yet she never dreamt of paying her debt to Mr. Craven.

Indeed, to do Miss Blake strict justice, she never thought of paying the debts she owed to anyone, unless she was obliged to do so.

Nowadays, I fear it would fare hard with her were she to try her old tactics with the British tradesman; but, in the time of which I am writing, co-operative societies were not, and then the British tradesman had no objection, I fancy, to be gulled.

Perhaps, like the lawyer and the unprofitable client, he set-off being gulled on one side his ledger against being fleeced on the other.

Be this as it may, we were always compounding some liability for Miss Blake, as well as letting her house and fighting with the tenants.

At first, as I have said, we found Miss Blake an awful bore, but we generally ended by deciding we could better spare a better man. Indeed, the months when she did not come to our office seemed to want flavour.

Of gratitude—popularly supposed to be essentially characteristic of the Irish—Miss Blake was utterly destitute. I never did know—I have never known since, so ungrateful a woman.

Not merely did she take everything Mr. Craven did for her as a right, but she absolutely turned the tables, and brought him in her debtor.

Once, only once, that I can remember, he ventured to ask when it would be convenient for her to repay some of the money he had from time to time advanced.

Miss Blake was taken by surprise, but she rose equal to the occasion.

"You are joking, Mr. Craven," she said. "You mean, when will I want to ask you to give me a share of the profits you have made out of the estate of my poor sister's husband. Why, that house has been as good as an annuity to you. For six long years it has stood empty, or next to empty, and never been out of law all the time."

"But, you know, Miss Blake, that not a shilling of profit has accrued to me from the house being in law," he pleaded. "I have always been too glad to get the rent for you, to insist upon my costs, and, really—."

"Now, do not try to impose upon me," she interrupted, "because it is of no use. Didn't you make thousands of the dead man, and now haven't you got the house? Why, if you never had a penny of costs, instead of all you have pocketed, that house and the name it has brought to you, and the fame which has spread abroad in consequence, can't be reckoned as less than hundreds a year to your firm. And yet you ask me for the return of a trumpery four or five sovereigns—I am ashamed of you! But I won't imitate your bad example. Let me have five more to-day, and you can stop ten out of the Colonel's first payment."

"I am very sorry," said my employer, "but I really have not five pounds

8

to spare."

"Hear him," remarked Miss Blake, turning towards me. "Young man"—Miss Blake steadily refused to recognise the possibility of any clerk being even by accident a gentleman—"will you hand me over the newspaper?"

I had not the faintest idea what she wanted with the newspaper, and neither had Mr. Craven, till she sat down again deliberately—the latter part of this conversation having taken place after she rose, preparatory to saying farewell—opened the sheet out to its full width, and commenced to read the debates.

"My dear Miss Blake," began Mr. Craven, after a minute's pause, "you know my time, when it is mine, is always at your disposal, but at the present moment several clients are waiting to see me, and—"

"Let them wait," said Miss Blake, as he hesitated a little. "Your time and their time is no more valuable than mine, and I mean to stay here," emphasising the word, "till you let me have that five pounds. Why, look, now, that house is taken on a two years' agreement, and you won't see me again for that time—likely as not, never; for who can tell what may happen to anybody in foreign parts? Only one charge I lay upon you, Mr. Craven: don't let me be buried in a strange country. It is bad enough to be so far as this from my father and my mother's remains, but I daresay I'll manage to rest in the same grave as my sister, though Robert Elmsdale lies between. He separated us in life—not that she ever cared for him; but it won't matter much when we are all bones and dust together—"

"If I let you have that five pounds," here broke in Mr. Craven, "do I clearly understand that I am to recoup myself out of Colonel Morris' first payment?"

"I said so as plain as I could speak," agreed Miss Blake; and her speech was very plain indeed.

Mr. Craven lifted his eyebrows and shrugged his shoulders, while he drew his cheque-book towards him.

"How is Helena?" he asked, as he wrote the final legendary flourish after Craven and Son.

"Helena is but middling, poor dear," answered Miss Blake—on that occasion she called her niece Hallana. "She frets, the creature, as is natural; but she will get better when we leave England. England is a hard country for anyone who is all nairves like Halana."

"Why do you never bring her to see me?" asked Mr. Craven, folding up the cheque.

"Bring her to be stared at by a parcel of clerks!" exclaimed Miss Blake, in a tone which really caused my hair to bristle. "Well-mannered, decent young fellows in their own rank, no doubt, but not fit to look at my sister's child. Now, now, Mr. Craven, ought Kathleen Blake's—or, rather, Kathleen Elmsdale's daughter to serve as a fifth of November guy for London lads? You know she is handsome enough to be a duchess, like her mother."

"Yes, yes, I know," agreed Mr. Craven, and handed over the cheque.

After I had held the door open for Miss Blake to pass out, and closed it securely and resumed my seat, Miss Blake turned the handle and treated us to another sight of her bonnet.

"Good-bye, William Craven, for two years at any rate; and if I never see you again, God bless you, for you've been a true friend to me and that poor child who has nobody else to look to," and then, before Mr. Craven could cross the room, she was gone.

"I wonder," said I, "if it will be two years before we see her again?"

"No, nor the fourth of two years," answered my employer. "There is something queer about that house."

"You don't think it is haunted, sir, do you?" I ventured.

"Of course not," said Mr. Craven, irritably; "but I do think some one wants to keep the place vacant, and is succeeding admirably."

The question I next put seemed irrelevant, but really resulted from a long train of thought. This was it:

"Is Miss Elmsdale very handsome, sir?"

"She is very beautiful," was the answer; "but not so beautiful as her mother was."

Ah me! two old, old stories in a sentence. He had loved the mother, and he did not love the daughter. He had seen the mother in his bright,

10

hopeful youth, and there was no light of morning left for him in which he could behold the child.

To other eyes she might, in her bright spring-time, seem lovely as an angel from heaven, but to him no more such visions were to be vouchsafed.

If beauty really went on decaying, as the ancients say, by this time there could be no beauty left. But oh! greybeard, the beauty remains, though our eyes may be too dim to see it; the beauty, the grace, the rippling laughter, and the saucy smiles, which once had power to stir to their very depths our hearts, friend—our hearts, yours and mine, comrade, feeble, and cold, and pulseless now.

THE CORONER'S INQUEST

The story was told to me afterwards, but I may as well weave it in with mine at this juncture.

From the maternal ancestress, the Demoiselles Blake inherited a certain amount of money. It was through no fault of the paternal Blake— through no want of endeavours on his part to make ducks and drakes of all fortune which came in his way, that their small inheritance remained intact; but the fortune was so willed that neither the girls nor he could divert the peaceful tenure of its half-yearly dividends.

The mother died first, and the father followed her ere long, and then the young ladies found themselves orphans, and the possessors of a fixed income of one hundred and thirty pounds a year.

A modest income, and yet, as I have been given to understand, they might have married well for the money.

In those days, particularly in Ireland, men went very cheap, and the Misses Blake, one and both, could, before they left off mourning, have wedded, respectively, a curate, a doctor, a constabulary officer, and the captain of a government schooner.

The Misses Blake looked higher, however, and came to England, where rich husbands are presumably procurable. Came, but missed their market. Miss Kathleen found only one lover, William Craven, whose honest affection she flouted; and Miss Susannah found no lover at all.

Miss Kathleen wanted a duke, or an earl—a prince of the blood royal being about that time unprocurable; and an attorney, to her Irish ideas, seemed a very poor sort of substitute. For which reason she rejected the attorney with scorn, and remained single, the while dukes and earls were marrying and intermarrying with their peers or their inferiors.

Then suddenly there came a frightful day when Kathleen and Susannah learned they were penniless, when they understood their trustee had robbed them, as he had robbed others, and had been paying their interest out of what was left of their principal.

They tried teaching, but they really had nothing to teach. They tried letting lodgings. Even lodgers rebelled against their untidiness and want of punctuality.

The eldest was very energetic and very determined, and the youngest very pretty and very conciliatory. Nevertheless, business is business, and lodgings are lodgings, and the Misses Blake were on the verge of beggary, when Mr. Elmsdale proposed for Miss Kathleen and was accepted.

Mr. Craven, by that time a family man, gave the bride away, and secured Mr. Elmsdale's business.

Possibly, had Mrs. Elmsdale's marriage proved happy, Mr. Craven might have soon lost sight of his former love. In matrimony, as in other matters, we are rarely so sympathetic with fulfilment as with disappointment. The pretty Miss Blake was a disappointed woman after she had secured Mr. Elmsdale. She then understood that the best life could offer her was something very different indeed from the ideal duke her beauty should have won, and she did not take much trouble to conceal her dissatisfaction with the arrangements of Providence.

Mr. Craven, seeing what Mr. Elmsdale was towards men, pitied her. Perhaps, had he seen what Mrs. Elmsdale was towards her husband, he might have pitied him; but, then, he did not see, for women are wonderful dissemblers.

There was Elmsdale, bluff in manner, short in person, red in the face, cumbersome in figure, addicted to naughty words, not nice about driving fearfully hard bargains, a man whom men hated, not undeservedly; and yet, nevertheless, a man capable of loving a woman with all the veins of his heart, and who might, had any woman been found to love him, have compassed earthly salvation.

There were those who said he never could compass eternal; but they chanced to be his debtors—and, after all, that question lay between himself and God. The other lay between himself and his wife, and it must be confessed, except so far as his passionate, disinterested love for an utterly selfish woman tended to redeem and humanise his nature, she never helped him one step along the better path.

But, then, the world could not know this, and Mr. Craven, of whom I

13

am speaking at the moment, was likely, naturally, to think Mr. Elmsdale all in the wrong.

On the one hand he saw the man as he appeared to men: on the other he saw the woman as she appeared to men, beautiful to the last; fragile, with the low voice, so beautiful in any woman, so more especially beautiful in an Irish woman; with a languid face which insured compassion while never asking for it; with the appearance of a martyr, and the tone and the manner of a suffering saint.

Everyone who beheld the pair together, remarked, "What a pity it was such a sweet creature should be married to such a bear!" but Mr. Elmsdale was no bear to his wife: he adored her. The selfishness, the discontent, the ill-health, as much the consequence of a peevish, petted temper, as of disease, which might well have exhausted the patience and tired out the love of a different man, only endeared her the more to him.

She made him feel how inferior he was to her in all respects; how tremendously she had condescended, when she agreed to become his wife; and he quietly accepted her estimation of him, and said with a humility which was touching from its simplicity:

"I know I am not worthy of you, Kathleen, but I do my best to make you happy."

For her sake, not being a liberal man, he spent money freely; for her sake he endured Miss Blake; for her sake he bought the place which afterwards caused us so much trouble; for her sake, he, who had always scoffed at the folly of people turning their houses into stores for "useless timber," as he styled the upholsterer's greatest triumphs, furnished his rooms with a lavish disregard of cost; for her sake, he, who hated society, smiled on visitors, and entertained the guests she invited, with no grudging hospitality. For her sake he dressed well, and did many other things which were equally antagonistic to his original nature; and he might just as well have gone his own way, and pleased himself only, for all the pleasure he gave her, or all the thanks she gave him.

If Mr. Elmsdale had come home drunk five evenings a week, and beaten his wife, and denied her the necessaries of life, and kept her purse in a chronic state of emptiness, she might very possibly have been extremely grateful for an occasional kind word or smile; but, as matters stood, Mrs. Elmsdale was not in the least grateful for a devotion, as beautiful as it was extraordinary, and posed herself on the domestic sofa in the character of a martyr.

Most people accepted the representation as true, and pitied her. Miss Blake, blissfully forgetful of that state of impecuniosity from which Mr. Elmsdale's proposal had extricated herself and her sister, never wearied of stating that "Katty had thrown herself away, and that Mr. Elmsdale was not fit to tie her shoe-string."

She generously admitted the poor creature did his best; but, according to Blake, the poor creature's best was very bad indeed.

"It's not his fault, but his misfortune," the lady was wont to remark, "that he's like dirt beside her. He can't help his birth, and his dragging-up, and his disreputable trade, or business, or whatever he likes to call it; he can't help never having had a father nor mother to speak of, and not a lady or gentleman belonging to the family since it came into existence. I'm not blaming him, but it is hard for Kathleen, and she reared as she was, and accustomed to the best society in Ireland,—which is very different, let me tell you, from the best anybody ever saw in England."

There were some who thought, if Mrs. Elmsdale could tolerate her sister's company, she might without difficulty have condoned her husband's want of acquaintance with some points of grammar and etiquette; and who said, amongst themselves, that whereas he only maltreated, Miss Blake mangled every letter in the alphabet; but these carping critics were in the minority.

Mrs. Elmsdale was a beauty, and a martyr; Mr. Elmsdale a rough beast, who had no capacity of ever developing into a prince. Miss Blake was a model of sisterly affection, and if eccentric in her manner, and bewildering in the vagaries of her accent, well, most Irish people, the highest in rank not excepted, were the same. Why, there was Lord So-and-so, who stated at a public meeting that "roight and moight were not always convartible tarms"; and accepted the cheers and laughter which greeted his utterance as

15

evidence that he had said something rather neat.

Miss Blake's accent was a very different affair indeed from those wrestles with his foe in which her brother-in-law always came off worsted. He endured agonies in trying to call himself Elmsdale, and rarely succeeded in styling his wife anything except Mrs. HE. I am told Miss Blake's mimicry of this peculiarity was delicious: but I never was privileged to hear her delineation, for, long before the period when this story opens, Mr. Elmsdale had departed to that land where no confusion of tongues can much signify, and where Helmsdale no doubt served his purpose just as well as Miss Blake's more refined pronunciation of his name.

Further, Miss Helena Elmsdale would not allow a word in depreciation of her father to be uttered when she was near, and as Miss Helena could on occasion develop a very pretty little temper, as well as considerable power of satire, Miss Blake dropped out of the habit of ridiculing Mr. Elmsdale's sins of omission and commission, and contented herself by generally asserting that, as his manner of living had broken her poor sister's heart, so his manner of dying had broken her—Miss Blake's—heart.

"It is only for the sake of the orphan child I am able to hold up at all," she would tell us. "I would not have blamed him so much for leaving us poor, but it was hard and cruel to leave us disgraced into the bargain"; and then Miss Blake would weep, and the wag of the office would take out his handkerchief and ostentatiously wipe his eyes.

She often threatened to complain of that boy—a merry, mischievous young imp—to Mr. Craven; but she never did so. Perhaps because the clerks always gave her rapt attention; and an interested audience was very pleasant to Miss Blake.

Considering the nature of Mr. Elmsdale's profession, Miss Blake had possibly some reason to complain of the extremely unprofitable manner in which he cut up. He was what the lady described as "a dirty money-lender."

Heaven only knows how he drifted into his occupation; few men, I imagine, select such a trade, though it is one which seems to exercise an enormous fascination for those who have adopted it.

The only son of a very small builder who managed to leave a few

16

hundred pounds behind him for the benefit of Elmsdale, then clerk in a contractor's office, he had seen enough of the anxieties connected with his father's business to wash his hands of bricks and mortar.

Experience, perhaps, had taught him also that people who advanced money to builders made a very nice little income out of the capital so employed; and it is quite possible that some of his father's acquaintances, always in want of ready cash, as speculative folks usually are, offered such terms for temporary accommodation as tempted him to enter into the business of which Miss Blake spoke so contemptuously.

Be this as it may, one thing is certain—by the time Elmsdale was thirty he had established a very nice little connection amongst needy men: whole streets were mortgaged to him; terraces, nominally the property of some well-to-do builder, were virtually his, since he only waited the well-to-do builder's inevitable bankruptcy to enter into possession. He was not a sixty per cent man, always requiring some very much better security than "a name" before parting with his money; but still even twenty per cent, usually means ruin, and, as a matter of course, most of Mr. Elmsdale's clients reached that pleasant goal.

They could have managed to do so, no doubt, had Mr. Elmsdale never existed; but as he was in existence, he served the purpose for which it seemed his mother had borne him; and sooner or later—as a rule, sooner than later—assumed the shape of Nemesis to most of those who "did business" with him.

There were exceptions, of course. Some men, by the help of exceptional good fortune, roguery, or genius, managed to get out of Mr. Elmsdale's hands by other paths than those leading through Basinghall or Portugal Streets; but they merely proved the rule.

Notably amongst these fortunate persons may be mentioned a Mr. Harrison and a Mr. Harringford—'Arrison and 'Arringford, as Mr. Elmsdale called them, when he did not refer to them as the two Haitches.

Of these, the first-named, after a few transactions, shook the dust of Mr. Elmsdale's office off his shoes, sent him the money he owed by his lawyer, and ever after referred to Mr. Elmsdale as "that thief," "that scoundrel," that

17

"swindling old vagabond," and so forth; but, then, hard words break no bones, and Mr. Harrison was not very well thought of himself.

His remarks, therefore, did Mr. Elmsdale very little harm—a money-lender is not usually spoken of in much pleasanter terms by those who once have been thankful enough for his cheque; and the world in general does not attach a vast amount of importance to the opinions of a former borrower. Mr. Harrison did not, therefore, hurt or benefit his quondam friend to any appreciable extent; but with Mr. Harringford the case was different.

He and Elmsdale had been doing business together for years, "everything he possessed in the world," he stated to an admiring coroner's jury summoned to sit on Mr. Elmsdale's body and inquire into the cause of that gentleman's death—"everything he possessed in the world, he owed to the deceased. Some people spoke hardly of him, but his experience of Mr. Elmsdale enabled him to say that a kinder-hearted, juster, honester, or better-principled man never existed. He charged high interest, certainly, and he expected to be paid his rate; but, then, there was no deception about the matter: if it was worth a borrower's while to take money at twenty per cent, why, there was an end of the matter. Business men are not children," remarked Mr. Harringford, "and ought not to borrow money at twenty per cent, unless they can make thirty per cent, out of it." Personally, he had never paid Mr. Elmsdale more than twelve and a half or fifteen per cent.; but, then, their transactions were on a large scale. Only the day before Mr. Elmsdale's death—he hesitated a little over that word, and became, as the reporters said, "affected"—he had paid him twenty thousand pounds. The deceased told him he had urgent need of the money, and at considerable inconvenience he raised the amount. If the question were pressed as to whether he guessed for what purpose that sum was so urgently needed, he would answer it, of course; but he suggested that it should not be pressed, as likely to give pain to those who were already in terrible affliction.

Hearing which, the jury pricked up their ears, and the coroner's curiosity became so intense that he experienced some difficulty in saying, calmly, that, "as the object of his sitting there was to elicit the truth, however much he should regret causing distress to anyone, he must request

18

that Mr. Harringford, whose scruples did him honour, would keep back no fact tending to throw light upon so sad an affair."

Having no alternative after this but to unburden himself of his secret, Mr. Harringford stated that he feared the deceased had been a heavy loser at Ascot. Mr. Harringford, having gone to that place with some friends, met Mr. Elmsdale on the race-course. Expressing astonishment at meeting him there, Mr. Elmsdale stated he had run down to look after a client of his who he feared was going wrong. He said he did not much care to do business with a betting man. In the course of subsequent conversation, however, he told the witness he had some money on the favourite.

As frequently proves the case, the favourite failed to come in first: that was all Mr. Harringford knew about the matter. Mr. Elmsdale never mentioned how much he had lost—in fact, he never referred again, except in general terms, to their meeting. He stated, however, that he must have money, and that immediately; if not the whole amount, half, at all events. The witness found, however, he could more easily raise the larger than the smaller sum. There had been a little unpleasantness between him and Mr. Elmsdale with reference to the demand for money made so suddenly and so peremptorily, and he bitterly regretted having even for a moment forgotten what was due to so kind a friend.

He knew of no reason in the world why Mr. Elmsdale should have committed suicide. He was, in business, eminently a cautious man, and Mr. Harringford had always supposed him to be wealthy; in fact, he believed him to be a man of large property. Since the death of his wife, he had, however, noticed a change in him; but still it never crossed the witness's mind that his brain was in any way affected.

Miss Blake, who had to this point postponed giving her evidence, on account of the "way she was upset," was now able to tell a sympathetic jury and a polite coroner all she knew of the matter.

"Indeed," she began, "Robert Elmsdale had never been the same man since her poor sister's death; he mooned about, and would sit for half an hour at a time, doing nothing but looking at a faded bit of the dining-room carpet."

He took no interest in anything; if he was asked any questions about the garden, he would say, "What does it matter? she cannot see it now."

"Indeed, my lord," said Miss Blake, in her agitation probably confounding the coroner with the chief justice, "it was just pitiful to see the creature; I am sure his ways got to be heart-breaking."

"After my sister's death," Miss Blake resumed, after a pause, devoted by herself, the jury, and the coroner to sentiment, "Robert Elmsdale gave up his office in London, and brought his business home. I do not know why he did this. He would not, had she been living, because he always kept his trade well out of her sight, poor man. Being what she was, she could not endure the name of it, naturally. It was not my place to say he shouldn't do what he liked in his own house, and I thought the excitement of building a new room, and quarrelling with the builder, and swearing at the men, was good for him. He made a fireproof place for his papers, and he fitted up the office like a library, and bought a beautiful large table, covered with leather; and nobody to have gone in would have thought the room was used for business. He had a Turkey carpet on the floor, and chairs that slipped about on castors; and he planned a covered way out into the road, with a separate entrance for itself, so that none of us ever knew who went out or who came in. He kept his affairs secret as the grave."

"No," in answer to the coroner, who began to think Miss Blake's narrative would never come to an end. "I heard no shot: none of us did: we all slept away from that part of the house; but I was restless that night, and could not sleep, and I got up and looked out at the river, and saw a flare of light on it. I thought it odd he was not gone to bed, but took little notice of the matter for a couple of hours more, when it was just getting gray in the morning, and I looked out again, and still seeing the light, slipped on a dressing-wrapper and my slippers, and ran downstairs to tell him he would ruin his health if he did not go to his bed.

"When I opened the door I could see nothing; the table stood between me and him; but the gas was flaring away, and as I went round to put it out, I came across him lying on the floor. It never occurred to me he was dead; I thought he was in a fit, and knelt down to unloose his cravat, then I found he had gone.

"The pistol lay on the carpet beside him—and that," finished Miss Blake, "is all I have to tell."

When asked if she had ever known of his losing money by betting, she answered it was not likely he would tell her anything of that kind.

"He always kept his business to himself," she affirmed, "as is the way of most men."

In answer to other questions, she stated she never heard of any losses in business; there was plenty of money always to be had for the asking. He was liberal enough, though perhaps not so liberal latterly, as before his wife's death; she didn't know anything of the state of his affairs. Likely, Mr. Craven could tell them all about that.

Mr. Craven, however, proved unable to do so. To the best of his belief, Mr. Elmsdale was in very easy circumstances. He had transacted a large amount of business for him, but never any involving pecuniary loss or anxiety; he should have thought him the last man in the world to run into such folly as betting; he had no doubt Mrs. Elmsdale's death had affected him disastrously. He said more than once to witness, if it were not for the sake of his child, he should not care if he died that night.

All of which, justifying the jury in returning a verdict of "suicide while of unsound mind," they expressed their unanimous opinion to that effect—thus "saving the family the condemnation of felo de se" remarked Miss Blake.

The dead man was buried, the church service read over his remains, the household was put into mourning, the blinds were drawn up, the windows flung open, and the business of life taken up once more by the survivors.

OUR LAST TENANT

It is quite competent for a person so to manage his affairs, that, whilst understanding all about them himself, another finds it next to impossible to make head or tail of his position.

Mr. Craven found that Mr. Elmsdale had effected this feat; entries there were in his books, intelligible enough, perhaps, to the man who made them, but as so much Hebrew to a stranger.

He had never kept a business banking account; he had no regular journal or ledger; he seemed to have depended on memoranda, and vague and uncertain writings in his diary, both for memory and accuracy; and as most of his business had been conducted viva voce, there were few letters to assist in throwing the slightest light on his transactions.

Even from the receipts, however, one thing was clear, viz., that he had, since his marriage, spent a very large sum of money; spent it lavishly, not to say foolishly. Indeed, the more closely Mr. Craven looked into affairs, the more satisfied he felt that Mr. Elmsdale had committed suicide simply because he was well-nigh ruined.

Mortgage-deeds Mr. Craven himself had drawn up, were nowhere to be found; neither could one sovereign of the money Mr. Harringford paid be discovered.

Miss Blake said she believed "that Harringford had never paid at all"; but this was clearly proved to be an error of judgment on the part of that impulsive lady. Not merely did Harringford hold the receipt for the money and the mortgage-deeds cancelled, but the cheque he had given to the mortgagee bore the endorsement—"Robert Elmsdale"; while the clerk who cashed it stated that Mr. Elmsdale presented the order in person, and that to him he handed the notes.

Whatever he had done with the money, no notes were to be found; a diligent search of the strong room produced nothing more important than the discovery of a cash-box containing three hundred pounds; the title-deeds of River Hall—such being the modest name by which Mr. Elmsdale had elected to have his residence distinguished; the leases relating to some small cottages near Barnes; all the letters his wife had ever written to him; two locks of her hair, one given before marriage, the other cut after her death; a curl severed from the head of my "baby daughter"; quantities of receipts— and nothing more.

"I wonder he can rest in his grave," said Miss Blake, when at last she began to realize, in a dim sort of way, the position of affairs.

According to the River Hall servants' version, Mr. Elmsdale did anything rather than rest in his grave. About the time the new mourning had been altered to fit perfectly, a nervous housemaid, who began perhaps to find the house dull, mooted the question as to whether "master walked."

Within a fortnight it was decided in solemn conclave that master did; and further, that the place was not what it had been; and moreover, that in the future it was likely to be still less like what it had been.

There is a wonderful instinct in the lower classes, which enables them to comprehend, without actual knowledge, when misfortune is coming upon a house: and in this instance that instinct was not at fault.

Long before Mr. Craven had satisfied himself that his client's estate was a very poor one, the River Hall servants, one after another, had given notice to leave—indeed, to speak more accurately, they did not give notice, for they left; and before they left they took care to baptize the house with such an exceedingly bad name, that neither for love nor money could Miss Blake get a fresh "help" to stay in it for more than twenty-four hours.

First one housemaid was taken with "the shivers"; then the cook had "the trembles"; then the coachman was prepared to take his solemn affidavit, that, one night long after everyone in the house to his knowledge was in bed, he "see from his room above the stables, a light a-shining on the Thames, and the figures of one or more a passing and a repassing across the blind." More than this, a new page-boy declared that, on a certain evening, before he had been told there was anything strange about the house, he heard the door of the passage leading from the library into the side-road slam violently, and looking to see who had gone out by that unused entrance, failed to perceive sign of man, woman, or child, by the bright moonlight.

Moved by some feeling which he professed himself unable to "put a name on," he proceeded to the door in question, and found it barred, chained, and bolted. While he was standing wondering what it meant, he noticed the light as of gas shining from underneath the library door; but when he softly turned the handle and peeped in, the room was dark as the grave, and "like cold water seemed running down his back."

Further, he averred, as he stole away into the hall, there was a sound followed him as between a groan and a cry. Hearing which statement, an impressionable charwoman went into hysterics, and had to be recalled to her senses by a dose of gin, suggested and taken strictly as a medicine.

But no supply of spirituous liquors, even had Miss Blake been disposed to distribute anything of the sort, could induce servants after a time to remain in, or charwomen to come to, the house. It had received a bad name, and that goes even further in disfavour of a residence than it does against a man or woman.

Finally, Miss Blake's establishment was limited to an old creature almost doting and totally deaf, the advantages of whose presence might have been considered problematical; but, then, as Miss Blake remarked, "she was somebody."

"And now she has taken fright," proceeded the lady. "How anyone could make her hear their story, the Lord in heaven alone knows; and if there was anything to see, I am sure she is far too blind to see it; but she says she daren't stay. She does not want to see poor master again till she is dead herself."

"I have got a tenant for the house the moment you like to say you will leave it," said Mr. Craven, in reply. "He cares for no ghost that ever was manufactured. He has a wife with a splendid digestion, and several grown-up sons and daughters. They will soon clear out the shadows; and their father is willing to pay two hundred and fifty pounds a year."

"And you think there is really nothing more of any use amongst the papers?"

"I am afraid not—I am afraid you must face the worst."

"And my sister's child left no better off than a street beggar," suggested Miss Blake.

24

"Come, come," remonstrated Mr. Craven; "matters are not so bad as all that comes to. Upon three hundred a year, you can live very comfortable on the Continent; and—"

"We'll go," interrupted Miss Blake; "but it is hard lines—not that anything better could have been expected from Robert Elmsdale."

"Ah! dear Miss Blake, the poor fellow is dead. Remember only his virtues, and let his faults rest."

"I sha'n't have much to burden my memory with, then," retorted Miss Blake, and departed.

Her next letter to my principal was dated from Rouen; but before that reached Buckingham Street, our troubles had begun.

For some reason best known to himself, Mr. Treseby, the good-natured country squire possessed of a wife with an excellent digestion, at the end of two months handed us half a year's rent, and requested we should try to let the house for the remainder of his term, he, in case of our failure, continuing amenable for the rent. In the course of the three years we secured eight tenants, and as from each a profit in the way of forfeit accrued, we had not to trouble Mr. Treseby for any more money, and were also enabled to remit some small bonuses—which came to her, Miss Blake assured us, as godsends—to the Continent.

After that the place stood vacant for a time. Various care-takers were eager to obtain the charge of it, but I only remember one who was not eager to leave.

That was a night-watchman, who never went home except in the daytime, and then to sleep, and he failed to understand why his wife, who was a pretty, delicate little creature, and the mother of four small children, should quarrel with her bread and butter, and want to leave so fine a place.

He argued the matter with her in so practical a fashion, that the nearest magistrate had to be elected umpire between them.

The whole story of the place was repeated in court, and the night-watchman's wife, who sobbed during the entire time she stood in the witness-box, made light of her black eye and numerous bruises, but said, "Not if Tim murdered her, could she stay alone in the house another night."

25

To prevent him murdering her, he was sent to gaol for two months, and Mr. Craven allowed her eight shillings a week till Tim was once more a free man, when he absconded, leaving wife and children chargeable to the parish.

"A poor, nervous creature," said Mr. Craven, who would not believe that where gas was, any house could be ghost-ridden. "We must really try to let the house in earnest."

And we did try, and we did let, over, and over, and over again, always with a like result, till at length Mr. Craven said to me: "Do you know, Patterson, I really am growing very uneasy about that house on the Thames. I am afraid some evil-disposed person is trying to keep it vacant."

"It certainly is very strange," was the only remark I felt capable of making.

We had joked so much about the house amongst ourselves, and ridiculed Miss Blake and her troubles to such an extent, that the matter bore no serious aspect for any of us juniors.

"If we are not soon able to let it," went on Mr. Craven, "I shall advise Miss Blake to auction off the furniture and sell the place. We must not always have an uninhabited house haunting our offices, Patterson."

I shook my head in grave assent, but all the time I was thinking the day when that house ceased to haunt our offices, would be a very dreary one for the wags amongst our clerks. "Yes, I certainly shall advise Miss Blake to sell," repeated Mr. Craven, slowly.

Although a hard-working man, he was eminently slow in his ideas and actions.

There was nothing express about our dear governor; upon no special mental train did he go careering through life. Eminently he preferred the parliamentary pace: and I am bound to say the life-journey so performed was beautiful exceedingly, with waits not devoid of interest at little stations utterly outside his profession, with kindly talk to little children, and timid women, and feeble men; with a pleasant smile for most with whom he came in contact, and time for words of kindly advice which did not fall perpetually on stony ground, but which sometimes grew to maturity, and produced rich grain of which himself beheld the garnering.

Nevertheless, to my younger and quicker nature, he did seem often very tardy.

"Why not advise her now?" I asked.

"Ah! my boy," he answered, "life is very short, yet it is long enough to have no need in it for hurry."

The same day, Colonel Morris appeared in our office. Within a fortnight, that gallant officer was our tenant; within a month, Mrs. Morris, an exceedingly fine lady, with grown-up children, with very young children also, with ayahs, with native servants, with English servants, with a list of acquaintances such as one may read of in the papers the day after a Queen's drawing-room, took possession of the Uninhabited House, and, for about three months, peace reigned in our dominions.

Buckingham Street, as represented by us, stank in the nostrils of no human being.

So far we were innocent of offence, we were simply ordinary solicitors and clerks, doing as fully and truly as we knew how, an extremely good business at rates which yielded a very fair return to our principal.

The Colonel was delighted with the place, he kindly called to say; so was Mrs. Morris; so were the grown-up sons and daughters of Colonel and Mrs. Morris; and so, it is to be presumed, were the infant branches of the family.

The native servants liked the place because Mr. Elmsdale, in view of his wife's delicate health, had made the house "like an oven," to quote Miss Blake. "It was bad for her, I know," proceeded that lady, "but she would have her own way, poor soul, and he—well, he'd have had the top brick of the chimney of a ten-story house off, if she had taken a fancy for that article."

Those stoves and pipes were a great bait to Colonel Morris, as well as a source of physical enjoyment to his servants.

He, too, had married a woman who was not always easy to please; but River Hall did please her, as was natural, with its luxuries of heat, ease, convenience, large rooms opening one out of another, wide verandahs overlooking the Thames, staircases easy of ascent; baths, hot, cold, and shower; a sweet, pretty garden, conservatory with a door leading into it from the spacious hall, all exceedingly cheap at two hundred pounds a year.

Accordingly, at first, the Colonel was delighted with the place, and not the less so because Mrs. Morris was delighted with it, and because it was also so far from town, that he had a remarkably good excuse for frequently visiting his club.

Before the new-comers, local tradesmen bowed down and did worship.

Visitors came and visitors went, carriages appeared in shoals, and double-knocks were plentiful as blackberries. A fresh leaf had evidently been turned over at River Hall, and the place meant to give no more trouble for ever to Miss Blake, or Mr. Craven, or anybody. So, as I have said, three months passed. We had got well into the dog-days by that time; there was very little to do in the office. Mr. Craven had left for his annual holiday, which he always took in the company of his wife and daughters—a correct, but possibly a depressing, way of spending a vacation which must have been intended to furnish some social variety in a man's life; and we were all very idle, and all very much inclined to grumble at the heat, and length, and general slowness of the days, when one morning, as I was going out in order to send a parcel off to Mrs. Craven, who should I meet coming panting up the stairs but Miss Blake!

"Is that you, Patterson?" she gasped. I assured her it was I in the flesh, and intimated my astonishment at seeing her in hers.

"Why, I thought you were in France, Miss Blake," I suggested.

"That's where I have just come from," she said. "Is Mr. Craven in?" I told her he was out of town.

"Ay—that's where everybody can be but me," she remarked, plaintively. "They can go out and stay out, while I am at the beck and call of all the scum of the earth. Well, well, I suppose there will be quiet for me sometime, if only in my coffin."

As I failed to see that any consolatory answer was possible, I made no reply. I only asked:

"Won't you walk into Mr. Craven's office, Miss Blake?"

"Now, I wonder," she said, "what good you think walking into his

28

office will do me!"

Nevertheless, she accepted the invitation. I have, in the course of years, seen many persons suffering from heat, but I never did see any human being in such a state as Miss Blake was that day.

Her face was a pure, rich red, from temple to chin; it resembled nothing so much as a brick which had been out for a long time, first in the sun and the wind, and then in a succession of heavy showers of rain. She looked weather-beaten, and sun-burnt, and sprayed with salt-water, all at once. Her eyes were a lighter blue than I previously thought eyes could be. Her cheek-bones stood out more prominently than I had thought cheek-bones capable of doing. Her mouth—not quite a bad one, by the way—opened wider than any within my experience; and her teeth, white and exposed, were suggestive of a set of tombstones planted outside a stonemason's shop, or an upper and lower set exhibited at the entrance to a dentist's operating-room. Poor dear Miss Blake, she and those pronounced teeth parted company long ago, and a much more becoming set—which she got exceedingly cheap, by agreeing with the maker to "send the whole of the city of London to her, if he liked"—now occupy their place.

But on that especial morning they were very prominent. Everything, in fact, about the lady, or belonging to her, seemed exaggerated, as if the heat of the weather had induced a tropical growth of her mental and bodily peculiarities. Her bonnet was crooked beyond even the ordinary capacity of Miss Blake's head-gear; the strings were rolled up till they looked like ropes which had been knotted under her chin. A veil, as large and black as a pirate's flag, floated down her back; her shawl was at sixes and sevens; one side of her dress had got torn from the bodice, and trailed on the ground leaving a broadly-marked line of dust on the carpet. She looked as if she had no petticoats on; and her boots—those were the days ere side-springs and buttons obtained—were one laced unevenly, and the other tied on with a piece of ribbon.

As for her gloves, they were in the state we always beheld them; if she ever bought a new pair (which I do not believe), she never treated us to a sight of them till they had been long past decent service. They never were buttoned, to begin with; they had a wrinkled and haggard appearance, as if from extreme old age. If their colour had originally been lavender, they were always black with dirt; if black, they were white with wear.

As a bad job, she had, apparently, years before, given up putting a stitch in the ends of the fingers, when a stitch gave way; and the consequence was that we were perfectly familiar with Miss Blake's nails—and those nails looked as if, at an early period of her life, a hammer had been brought heavily down upon them. Mrs. Elmsdale might well be a beauty, for she had taken not only her own share of the good looks of the family, but her sister's also.

We used often, at the office, to marvel why Miss Blake ever wore a collar, or a tucker, or a frill, or a pair of cuffs. So far as clean linen was concerned, she would have appeared infinitely brighter and fresher had she and female frippery at once parted company. Her laces were always in tatters, her collars soiled, her cuffs torn, and her frills limp. I wonder what the natives thought of her in France! In London, we decided—and accurately, I believe—that Miss Blake, in the solitude of her own chamber, washed and got-up her cambrics and fine linen—and it was a "get-up" and a "put-on" as well.

Had any other woman, dressed like Miss Blake, come to our office, I fear the clerks would not have been over-civil to her. But Miss Blake was our own, our very own. She had grown to be as our very flesh and blood. We did not love her, but she was associated with us by the closest ties that can subsist between lawyer and client. Had anything happened to Miss Blake, we should, in the event of her death, have gone in a body to her funeral, and felt a want in our lives for ever after.

But Miss Blake had not the slightest intention of dying: we were not afraid of that calamity. The only thing we really did dread was that some day she might insist upon laying the blame of River Hall remaining uninhabited on our shoulders, and demand that Mr. Craven should pay her the rent out of his own pocket.

We knew if she took that, or any other pecuniary matter, seriously in hand, she would carry it through; and, between jest and earnest, we were wont to speculate whether, in the end, it might not prove cheaper to our firm if Mr. Craven were to farm that place, and pay Miss Blake's niece an annuity of say one hundred a year.

Ultimately we decided that it would, but that such a scheme was impracticable, because Miss Blake would always think we were making a fortune out of River Hall, and give us no peace till she had a share of the profit.

For a time, Miss Blake—after unfastening her bonnet-strings, and taking out her brooch and throwing back her shawl—sat fanning herself with a dilapidated glove, and saying, "Oh dear! oh dear! what is to become of me I cannot imagine." But, at length, finding I was not to be betrayed into questioning, she observed:

"If William Craven knew the distress I am in, he would not be out of town enjoying himself, I'll be bound."

"I am quite certain he would not," I answered, boldly. "But as he is away, is there nothing we can do for you?"

She shook her head mournfully. "You're all a parcel of boys and children together," was her comprehensive answer.

"But there is our manager, Mr. Taylor," I suggested.

"Him!" she exclaimed. "Now, if you don't want me to walk out of the office and never set foot in it again, don't talk to me about Taylor."

"Has Mr. Taylor offended you?" I ventured to inquire.

"Lads of your age should not ask too many questions," she replied. "What I have against Taylor is nothing to you; only don't make me desperate by mentioning his name."

I hastened to assure her that it should never be uttered by me again in her presence, and there ensued a pause, which she filled by looking round the office and taking a mental inventory of everything it contained.

Eventually, her survey ended in this remark, "And he can go out of town as well, and keep a brougham for his wife, and draw them daughters of his out like figures in a fashion-book, and my poor sister's child living in a two-pair lodging."

"I fear, Miss Blake," I ventured, "that something is the matter at River

Hall."

"You fear, do you, young man?" she returned. "You ought to get a first prize for guessing. As if anything else could ever bring me back to London."

"Can I be of no service to you in the matter?"

"I don't think you can, but you may as well see his letter." And diving into the depths of her pocket, she produced Colonel Morris' communication, which was very short, but very much to the purpose.

"Not wishing," he said, "to behave in any unhandsome manner, I send you herewith" (herewith meant the keys of River Hall and his letter) "a cheque for one half-year's rent. You must know that, had I been aware of the antecedents of the place, I should never have become your tenant; and I must say, considering I have a wife in delicate health, and young children, the deception practised by your lawyers in concealing the fact that no previous occupant has been able to remain in the house, seems most unpardonable. I am a soldier, and, to me, these trade tricks appear dishonourable. Still, as I understand your position is an exceptional one, I am willing to forgive the wrong which has been done, and to pay six months' rent for a house I shall no longer occupy. In the event of these concessions appearing insufficient, I beg to enclose the names of my solicitors, and have the honour, madam, to remain

"Your most obedient servant,

"HERCULES MORRIS."

In order to gain time, I read this letter twice over; then, diplomatically, as I thought, I said:

"What are you going to do, Miss Blake?"

"What are you going to do, is much nearer the point, I am thinking!" retorted that lady. "Do you imagine there is so much pleasure or profit in keeping a lawyer, that people want to do lawyer's work for themselves?"

Which really was hard upon us all, considering that so long as she could do her work for herself, Miss Blake ignored both Mr. Craven and his clerks.

Not a shilling of money would she ever, if she could help it, permit to

32

pass through our hands—not the slightest chance did she ever voluntarily give Mr. Craven of recouping himself those costs or loans in which her acquaintance involved her sister's former suitor.

Had he felt any inclination—which I am quite certain he never did—to deduct Miss Helena's indebtedness, as represented by her aunt, out of Miss Helena's income, he could not have done it. The tenant's money usually went straight into Miss Blake's hands.

What she did with it, Heaven only knows. I know she did not buy herself gloves!

Twirling the Colonel's letter about, I thought the position over.

"What, then," I asked, "do you wish us to do?"

Habited as I have attempted to describe, Miss Blake sat at one side of a library-table. In, I flatter myself, a decent suit of clothes, washed, brushed, shaved, I sat on the other. To ordinary observers, I know I must have seemed much the best man of the two—yet Miss Blake got the better of me.

She, that dilapidated, red-hot, crumpled-collared, fingerless-gloved woman, looked me over from head to foot, as I conceived, though my boots were hidden away under the table, and I declare—I swear—she put me out of countenance. I felt small under the stare of a person with whom I would not then have walked through Hyde Park in the afternoon for almost any amount of money which could have been offered to me.

"Though you are only a clerk," she said at length, apparently quite unconscious of the effect she had produced, "you seem a very decent sort of young man. As Mr. Craven is out of the way, suppose you go and see that Morris man, and ask him what he means by his impudent letter."

I rose to the bait. Being in Mr. Craven's employment, it is unnecessary to say I, in common with every other person about the place, thought I could manage his business for him very much better than he could manage it for himself; and it had always been my own personal conviction that if the letting of the Uninhabited House were entrusted to me, the place would not stand long empty.

Miss Blake's proposition was, therefore, most agreeable; but still, I did not at once swallow her hook. Mr. Craven, I felt, might scarcely approve of my taking it upon myself to call upon Colonel Morris while Mr. Taylor was able and willing to venture upon such a step, and I therefore suggested to our client the advisability of first asking Mr. Craven's opinion about the affair.

"And keep me in suspense while you are writing and answering and running up a bill as long as Midsummer Day," she retorted. "No, thank you. If you don't think my business worth your attention, I'll go to somebody that may be glad of it." And she began tying her strings and feeling after her shawl in a manner which looked very much indeed like carrying out her threat.

At that moment I made up my mind to consult Taylor as to what ought to be done. So I appeased Miss Blake by assuring her, in a diplomatic manner, that Colonel Morris should be visited, and promising to communicate the result of the interview by letter.

"That you won't," she answered. "I'll be here to-morrow to know what he has to say for himself. He is just tired of the house, like the rest of them, and wants to be rid of his bargain."

"I am not quite sure of that," I said, remembering my principal's suggestion. "It is strange, if there really is nothing objectionable about the house, that no one can be found to stay in it. Mr. Craven has hinted that he fancies some evil-disposed person must be playing tricks, in order to frighten tenants away."

"It is likely enough," she agreed. "Robert Elmsdale had plenty of enemies and few friends; but that is no reason why we should starve, is it?"

I failed to see the logical sequence of Miss Blake's remark, nevertheless I did not dare to tell her so; and agreed it was no reason why she and her niece should be driven into that workhouse which she frequently declared they "must come to."

"Remember," were her parting words, "I shall be here to-morrow morning early, and expect you to have good news for me."

Inwardly resolving not to be in the way, I said I hoped there would be good news for her, and went in search of Taylor.

"Miss Blake has been here," I began. "THE HOUSE is empty again.

34

Colonel Morris has sent her half a year's rent, the keys, and the address of his solicitors. He says we have acted disgracefully in the matter, and she wants me to go and see him, and declares she will be back here first thing to-morrow morning to know what he has to say for himself. What ought I to do?"

Before Mr. Taylor answered my question, he delivered himself of a comprehensive anathema which included Miss Blake, River Hall, the late owner, and ourselves. He further wished he might be essentially etceteraed if he believed there was another solicitor, besides Mr. Craven, in London who would allow such a hag to haunt his offices.

"Talk about River Hall being haunted," he finished; "it is we who are witch-ridden, I call it, by that old Irishwoman. She ought to be burnt at Smithfield. I'd be at the expense of the faggots!"

"What have you and Miss Blake quarrelled about?" I inquired. "You say she is a witch, and she has made me take a solemn oath never to mention your name again in her presence."

"I'd keep her presence out of these offices, if I was Mr. Craven," he answered. "She has cost us more than the whole freehold of River Hall is worth."

Something in his manner, more than in his words, made me comprehend that Miss Blake had borrowed money from him, and not repaid it, so I did not press for further explanation, but only asked him once again what I ought to do about calling upon Colonel Morris.

"Call, and be hanged, if you like!" was the reply; and as Mr. Taylor was not usually a man given to violent language, I understood that Miss Blake's name acted upon his temper with the same magical effect as a red rag does upon that of a turkey-cock.

MYSELF AND MISS BLAKE

Colonel Morris, after leaving River Hall, had migrated temporarily to a fashionable West End hotel, and was, when I called to see him, partaking of tiffin in the bosom of his family, instead of at his club.

As it was notorious that he and Mrs. Morris failed to lead the most harmonious of lives, I did not feel surprised to find him in an extremely bad temper.

In person, short, dapper, wiry, thin, and precise, his manner matched his appearance. He had martinet written on every square foot of his figure. His moustache was fiercely waxed, his shirt-collar inflexible, his backbone stiff, while his shoulder-blades met flat and even behind. He held his chin a little up in the air, and his walk was less a march than a strut.

He came into the room where I had been waiting for him, as I fancied he might have come on a wet, cold morning to meet an awkward-squad. He held the card I sent for his inspection in his hand, and referred to it, after he had looked me over with a supercilious glance.

"Mr. Patterson, from Messrs. Craven and Son," he read slowly out loud, and then added:

"May I inquire what Mr. Patterson from Messrs. Craven and Son wants with me?"

"I come from Miss Blake, sir," I remarked.

"It is here written that you come from Messrs. Craven and Son," he said.

"So I do, sir—upon Miss Blake's business. She is a client of ours, as you may remember."

"I do remember. Go on."

He would not sit down himself or ask me to be seated, so we stood throughout the interview. I with my hat in my hand, he twirling his moustache or scrutinising his nails while he talked.

"Miss Blake has received a letter from you, sir, and has requested me to ask you for an explanation of it."

"I have no further explanation to give," he replied.

"But as you took the house for two years, we cannot advise Miss Blake to allow you to relinquish possession in consideration of your having paid her six months' rent."

"Very well. Then you can advise her to fight the matter, as I suppose you will. I am prepared to fight it."

"We never like fighting, if a matter can be arranged amicably," I answered. "Mr. Craven is at present out of town; but I know I am only speaking his words, when I say we shall be glad to advise Miss Blake to accept any reasonable proposition which you may feel inclined to make."

"I have sent her half a year's rent," was his reply; "and I have refrained from prosecuting you all for conspiracy, as I am told I might have done. Lawyers, I am aware, admit they have no consciences, and I can make some allowance for a person in Miss Blake's position, otherwise."

"Yes, sir?" I said, interrogatively.

"I should never have paid one penny. It has, I find, been a well-known fact to Mr. Craven, as well as to Miss Blake, that no tenant can remain in River Hall. When my wife was first taken ill there—in consequence of the frightful shock she received—I sent for the nearest medical man, and he refused to come; absolutely sent me a note, saying, 'he was very sorry, but he must decline to attend Mrs. Morris. Doubtless, she had her own physician, who would be happy to devote himself to the case.'"

"And what did you do?" I asked, my pulses tingling with awakened curiosity.

"Do!" he repeated, pleased, perhaps, to find so appreciative a listener. "I sent, of course, for the best advice to be had in London, and I went to the local doctor—a man who keeps a surgery and dispenses medicines—myself, to ask what he meant by returning such an insolent message in answer to my summons. And what do you suppose he said by way of apology?"

"I cannot imagine," I replied.

"He said he would not for ten times over the value of all the River Hall patients, attend a case in the house again. 'No person can live in it,' he went on, 'and keep his, her, or its health. Whether it is the river, or the drains, or the late owner, or the devil, I have not an idea. I can only tell you no one has

37

been able to remain in it since Mr. Elmsdale's death, and if I attend a case there, of course I say, Get out of this at once. Then comes Miss Blake and threatens me with assault and battery—swears she will bring an action against me for libelling the place; declares I wish to drive her and her niece to the workhouse, and asserts I am in league with some one who wants to keep the house vacant, and I am sick of it. Get what doctor you choose, but don't send for me.'"

"Well, sir?" I suggested.

"Well! I don't consider it well at all. Here am I, a man returning to his native country—and a beastly country it is!—after nearly thirty years' absence, and the first transaction upon which I engage proves a swindle. Yes, a swindle, Mr. Patterson. I went to you in all good faith, took that house at your own rent, thought I had got a desirable home, and believed I was dealing with respectable people, and now I find I was utterly deceived, both as regards the place and your probity. You knew the house was uninhabitable, and yet you let it to me."

"I give you my word," I said, "that we really do not know yet in what way the house is uninhabitable. It is a good house, as you know; it is well furnished; the drainage is perfect; so far as we are concerned, we do not believe a fault can be found with the place. Still, it has been a fact that tenants will not stay in it, and we were therefore glad to let it to a gentleman like yourself, who would, we expected, prove above subscribing to that which can only be a vulgar prejudice."

"What is a vulgar prejudice?" he asked.

"The idea that River Hall is haunted," I replied.

"River Hall is haunted, young man," he said, solemnly.

"By what?" I asked.

"By some one who cannot rest in his grave," was the answer.

"Colonel Morris," I said, "some one must be playing tricks in the house."

"If so, that some one does not belong to this world," he remarked.

"Do you mean really and seriously to tell me you believe in ghosts?" I asked, perhaps a little scornfully.

38

"I do, and if you had lived in River Hall, you would believe in them too," he replied. "I will tell you," he went on, "what I saw in the house myself. You know the library?"

I nodded in assent. We did know the library. There our trouble seemed to have taken up its abode.

"Are you aware lights have frequently been reflected from that room, when no light has actually been in it?"

I could only admit this had occasionally proved a ground of what we considered unreasonable complaint.

"One evening," went on the Colonel, "I determined to test the matter for myself. Long before dusk I entered the room and examined it thoroughly—saw to the fastenings of the windows, drew up the blinds, locked the door, and put the key in my pocket. After dinner I took a cigar and walked up and down the grass path beside the river, until dark. There was no light—not a sign of light of any kind, as I turned once more and walked up the path again; but as I was retracing my steps I saw that the room was brilliantly illuminated. I rushed to the nearest window and looked in. The gas was all ablaze, the door of the strong room open, the table strewed with papers, while in an office-chair drawn close up to the largest drawer, a man was seated counting over bank-notes. He had a pile of them before him, and I distinctly saw that he wetted his fingers in order to separate them."

"Most extraordinary!" I exclaimed. I could not decently have said anything less; but I confess that I had in my recollection the fact of Colonel Morris having dined.

"The most extraordinary part of the story is still to come," he remarked. "I hurried at once into the house, unlocked the door, found the library in pitch darkness, and when I lit the gas the strong room was closed; there was no office-chair in the room, no papers were on the table—everything, in fact, was precisely in the same condition as I had left it a few hours before. Now, no person in the flesh could have performed such a feat as that."

"I cannot agree with you there," I ventured. "It seems to me less difficult to believe the whole thing a trick, than to attribute the occurrence to supernatural agency. In fact, while I do not say it is impossible for ghosts to be, I cannot accept the fact of their existence."

"Well, I can, then," retorted the Colonel. "Why, sir, once at the Cape of Good Hope—" but there he paused. Apparently he recollected just in time that the Cape of Good Hope was a long way from River Hall.

"And Mrs. Morris," I suggested, leading him back to the banks of the Thames. "You mentioned some shock—"

"Yes," he said, frankly. "She met the same person on the staircase I saw in the library. He carried in one hand a lighted candle, and in the other a bundle of bank-notes. He never looked at her as he passed—never turned his head to the spot where she stood gazing after him in a perfect access of terror, but walked quietly downstairs, crossed the hall, and went straight into the library without opening the door. She fainted dead away, and has never known an hour's good health since."

"According to all accounts, she had not before, or good temper either," I thought; but I only said, "You had told Mrs. Morris, I presume, of your adventure in the library?"

"No," he answered; "I had not; I did not mention it to anyone except a brother officer, who dined with me the next evening."

"Your conversation with him might have been overheard, I suppose," I urged.

"It is possible, but scarcely probable," he replied. "At all events, I am quite certain it never reached my wife's ears, or she would not have stayed another night in the house."

I stood for a few moments irresolute, but then I spoke. I told him how much we—meaning Messrs. Craven and Son—his manager and his cashier, and his clerks, regretted the inconvenience to which he had been put; delicately I touched upon the concern we felt at hearing of Mrs. Morris' illness. But, I added, I feared his explanation, courteous and ample as it had been, would not satisfy Miss Blake, and trusted he might, upon consideration, feel disposed to compromise the matter.

"We," I added, "will be only too happy to recommend our client to accept any reasonable proposal you may think it well to make."

40

Whereupon it suddenly dawned upon the Colonel that he had been showing me all his hand, and forthwith he adopted a very natural course. He ordered me to leave the room and the hotel, and not to show my face before him again at my peril. And I obeyed his instructions to the letter.

On the same evening of that day I took a long walk round by the Uninhabited House.

There it was, just as I had seen it last, with high brick walls dividing it from the road; with its belt of forest-trees separating it from the next residence, with its long frontage to the river, with its closed gates and shuttered postern-door.

The entrance to it was not from the main highway, but from a lane which led right down to the Thames; and I went to the very bottom of that lane and swung myself by means of a post right over the river, so that I might get a view of the windows of the room with which so ghostly a character was associated. The blinds were all down and the whole place looked innocent enough.

The strong, sweet, subtle smell of mignonette came wafted to my senses, the odours of jessamine, roses, and myrtle floated to me on the evening breeze. I could just catch a glimpse of the flower-gardens, radiant with colour, full of leaf and bloom.

"No haunted look there," I thought. "The house is right enough, but some one must have determined to keep it empty." And then I swung myself back into the lane again, and the shadow of the high brick wall projected itself across my mind as it did across my body.

"Is this place to let again, do you know?" said a voice in my ear, as I stood looking at the private door which gave a separate entrance to that evil-reputed library.

The question was a natural one, and the voice not unpleasant, yet I started, having noticed no one near me.

"I beg your pardon," said the owner of the voice. "Nervous, I fear!"

"No, not at all, only my thoughts were wandering. I beg your pardon— I do not know whether the place is to let or not."

"A good house?" This might have been interrogative, or uttered as an

41

assertion, but I took it as the former, and answered accordingly.

"Yes, a good house—a very good house, indeed," I said.

"It is often vacant, though," he said, with a light laugh.

"Through no fault of the house," I added.

"Oh! it is the fault of the tenants, is it?" he remarked, laughing once more. "The owners, I should think, must be rather tired of their property by this time."

"I do not know that," I replied. "They live in hope of finding a good and sensible tenant willing to take it."

"And equally willing to keep it, eh?" he remarked. "Well, I, perhaps, am not much of a judge in the matter, but I should say they will have to wait a long time first."

"You know something about the house?" I said, interrogatively.

"Yes," he answered, "most people about here do, I fancy—but least said soonest mended"; and as by this time we had reached the top of the lane, he bade me a civil good-evening, and struck off in a westerly direction.

Though the light of the setting sun shone full in my face, and I had to shade my eyes in order to enable me to see at all, moved by some feeling impossible to analyse, I stood watching that retreating figure. Afterwards I could have sworn to the man among ten thousand.

A man of about fifty, well and plainly dressed, who did not appear to be in ill-health, yet whose complexion had a blanched look, like forced sea-kale; a man of under, rather than over middle height, not of slight make, but lean as if the flesh had been all worn off his bones; a man with sad, anxious, outlooking, abstracted eyes, with a nose slightly hooked, without a trace of whisker, with hair thin and straight and flaked with white, active and lithe in his movements, a swift walker, though he had a slight halt. While looking at him thrown up in relief against the glowing western sky, I noticed, what had previously escaped my attention, that he was a little deformed. His right shoulder was rather higher than the other. A man with a story in his memory, I imagined; a man who had been jilted by the girl he loved, or who had lost her by death, or whose wife had proved faithless; whose life, at all events, had been marred by a great trouble. So, in my folly, I decided; for I was

42

young then, and romantic, and had experienced some sorrow myself connected with pecuniary matters.

For the latter reason, it never perhaps occurred to me to associate the trouble of my new acquaintance, if he could be so called, with money annoyances. I knew, or thought I knew, at all events, the expression loss of fortune stamps on a man's face; and the look which haunted me for days after had nothing in it of discontent, or self-assertion, or struggling gentility, or vehement protest against the decrees of fortune. Still less was it submissive. As I have said, it haunted me for days, then the memory grew less vivid, then I forgot the man altogether. Indeed, we shortly became so absorbed in the fight between Miss Blake and Colonel Morris, that we had little time to devote to the consideration of other matters.

True to her promise, Miss Blake appeared next morning in Buckingham Street. Without bestowing upon me even the courtesy of "good morning," she plunged into the subject next her heart.

"Did you see him?" she asked.

I told her I had. I repeated much of what he said; I assured her he was determined to fight the matter, and that although I did really not think any jury would give a verdict in his favour, still I believed, if the matter came into court, it would prevent our ever letting the house again.

"I should strongly recommend you, Miss Blake," I finished, "to keep what he offers, and let us try and find another tenant."

"And who asked you to recommend anything, you fast young man?" she demanded. "I am sure I did not, and I am very sure Mr. Craven would not be best pleased to know his clerks were setting themselves up higher than their master. You would never find William Craven giving himself airs such as you young whipper-snappers think make you seem of some consequence. I just tell him what I want done, and he does it, and you will please to do the same, and serve a writ on that villain without an hour's delay."

I asked on what grounds we were to serve the writ. I pointed out that Colonel Morris did not owe her a penny, and would not owe her a penny for some months to come; and in reply she said she would merely inquire if I

43

meant that she and her poor niece were to go to the workhouse.

To this I answered that the amount already remitted by Colonel Morris would prevent such a calamity, but she stopped my attempt at consolation by telling me not to talk about things I did not understand.

"Give me William Craven's address," she added, "and I will write to him direct. I wonder what he means by leaving a parcel of ignorant boys to attend to his clients while he is away enjoying himself! Give me his address, and some paper and an envelope, and I can write my letter here."

I handed her the paper and the envelope, and placed pen and ink conveniently before her, but I declined to give her Mr. Craven's address. We would forward the letter, I said; but when Mr. Craven went away for his holiday, he was naturally anxious to leave business behind as much as possible.

Then Miss Blake took steady aim, and fired at me. Broadside after broadside did she pour into my unprotected ears; she opened the vials of her wrath and overwhelmed me with reproaches; she raked up all the grievances she had for years been cherishing against England, and by some sort of verbal legerdemain made me responsible for every evil she could recollect as ever having happened to her. Her sister's marriage, her death, Mr. Elmsdale's suicide, the unsatisfactory state of his affairs, the prejudice against River Hall, the defection of Colonel Morris—all these things she laid at my door, and insisted on making me responsible for them.

"And now," she finished, pushing back her bonnet and pulling off her gloves, "I'll just write my opinion of you to Mr. Craven, and I'll wait till you direct the envelope, and I'll go with you to the post, and I'll see you put the letter in the box. If you and your fine Colonel Morris think you can frighten or flatter me, you are both much mistaken, I can tell you that!"

I did not answer her. I was too greatly affronted to express what I felt in words. I sat on the other side of the table—for I would not leave her alone in Mr. Craven's office—sulking, while she wrote her letter, which she did in a great, fat, splashing sort of hand, with every other word underlined; and when she had done, and tossed the missive over to me, I directed it, took my hat, and prepared to accompany her to the Charing Cross office.

We went down the staircase together in silence, up Buckingham Street, across the Strand, and so to Charing Cross, where she saw me drop the letter into the box. All this time we did not exchange a syllable, but when, after raising my hat, I was about to turn away, she seized hold of my arm, and said, "Don't let us part in bad blood. Though you are only a clerk, you have got your feelings, no doubt, and if in my temper I hurt them, I am sorry. Can I say more? You are a decent lad enough, as times go in England, and my bark is worse than my bite. I didn't write a word about you to William Craven. Shake hands, and don't bear malice to a poor lonely woman."

Thus exhorted, I took her hand and shook it, and then, in token of entire amity, she told me she had forgotten to bring her purse with her and could I let her have a sovereign. She would pay me, she declared solemnly, the first day she came again to the office.

This of course I did not believe in the least, nevertheless I gave her what she required—and Heaven knows, sovereigns were scarce enough with me then—thankfully, and felt sincerely obliged to her for making herself my debtor. Miss Blake did sometimes ruffle one's feathers most confoundedly, and yet I knew it would have grieved me had we parted in enmity.

Sometimes, now, when I look upon her quiet and utterly respectable old age—when I contemplate her pathetic grey hair and conventional lace cap—when I view her clothed like other people and in her right mind, I am very glad indeed to remember I had no second thought about that sovereign, but gave it to her—with all the veins of my heart, as she would have emphasised the proceeding.

"Though you have no name to speak of," observed Miss Blake as she pocketed the coin, "I think there must be some sort of blood in you. I knew Pattersons once who were connected by marriage with a great duke in the west of Ireland. Can you say if by chance you can trace relationship to any of them?"

"I can say most certainly not, Miss Blake," I replied. "We are Pattersons of nowhere and relations of no one."

"Well, well," remarked the lady, pityingly, "you can't help that, poor lad. And if you attend to your duties, you may yet be a rich City alderman."

With which comfort she left me, and wended her homeward way through St. Martin's Lane and the Seven Dials.

THE TRIAL

Next day but one Mr. Craven astonished us all by walking into the office about ten o'clock. He looked stout and well, sunburnt to a degree, and all the better physically for his trip to the seaside. We were unfeignedly glad to see him. Given a good employer, and it must be an extremely bad employé who rejoices in his absence. If we were not saints, we were none of us very black sheep, and accordingly, from the porter to the managing clerk, our faces brightened at sight of our principal.

But after the first genial "how are you" and "good morning," Mr. Craven's face told tales: he had come back out of sorts. He was vexed about Miss Blake's letter, and, astonishing to relate, he was angry with me for having called upon Colonel Morris.

"You take too much upon you, Patterson," he remarked. "It is a growing habit with you, and you must try to check it."

I did not answer him by a word; my heart seemed in my mouth; I felt as if I was choking. I only inclined my head in token that I heard and understood, and assented; then, having, fortunately, work to attend to out of doors, I seized an early opportunity of slipping down the staircase and walking off to Chancery Lane. When I returned, after hours, to Buckingham Street, one of the small boys in the outer office told me I was to go to Mr. Craven's room directly.

"You'll catch it," remarked the young fiend. "He has asked for you a dozen times, at least."

"What can be wrong now?" I thought, as I walked straight along the passage to Mr. Craven's office.

"Patterson," he said, as I announced my return.

"Yes, sir?"

"I spoke hastily to you this morning, and I regret having done so."

"Oh! sir," I cried. And that was all. We were better friends than ever. Do you wonder that I liked my principal? If so, it is only because I am unable to portray him as he really was. The age of chivalry is past; but still it is no exaggeration to say I would have died cheerfully if my dying could

47

have served Mr. Craven.

Life holds me now by many and many a nearer and dearer tie than was the case in those days so far and far away; nevertheless, I would run any risk, encounter any peril, if by so doing I could serve the man who in my youth treated me with a kindness far beyond my deserts.

He did not, when he came suddenly to town in this manner, stop at his own house, which was, on such occasions, given over to charwomen and tradespeople of all descriptions; but he put up at an old-fashioned family hotel where, on that especial evening, he asked me to dine with him.

Over dessert he opened his mind to me on the subject of the "Uninhabited House." He said the evil was becoming one of serious magnitude. He declared he could not imagine what the result might prove. "With all the will in the world," he said, "to assist Miss Blake and that poor child, I cannot undertake to provide for them. Something must be done in the affair, and I am sure I cannot see what that something is to be. Since Mr. Elmsdale bought the place, the neighbourhood has gone down. If we sold the freehold as it stands, I fear we should not get more than a thousand pounds for it, and a thousand pounds would not last Miss Blake three years; as for supposing she could live on the interest, that is out of the question. The ground might be cut up and let for business purposes, of course, but that would be a work of time. I confess, I do not know what to think about the matter or how to act in it."

"Do you suppose the place really is haunted?" I ventured to inquire.

"Haunted?—pooh! nonsense," answered Mr. Craven, pettishly. "Do I suppose this room is haunted; do I believe my offices are haunted? No sane man has faith in any folly of the kind; but the place has got a bad name; I suspect it is unhealthy, and the tenants, when they find that out, seize on the first excuse which offers. It is known we have compromised a good many tenancies, and I am afraid we shall have to fight this case, if only to show we do not intend being patient for ever. Besides, we shall exhaust the matter: we shall hear what the ghost-seers have to say for themselves on oath. There is little doubt of our getting a verdict, for the British juryman is, as a rule, not imaginative."

"I think we shall get a verdict," I agreed; "but I fancy we shall never get another tenant."

"There are surely as good fish in the sea as ever came out of it," he answered, with a smile; "and we shall come across some worthy country squire, possessed of pretty daughters, who will be delighted to find so cheap and sweet a nest for his birds, when they want to be near London."

"I wish sir," I said, "you would see Colonel Morris yourself. I am quite certain that every statement he made to me is true in his belief. I do not say, I believe him; I only say, what he told me justifies the inference that some one is playing a clever game in River Hall," and then I repeated in detail all the circumstances Colonel Morris had communicated to me, not excepting the wonderful phenomenon witnessed by Mr. Morris, of a man walking through a closed door.

Mr. Craven listened to me in silence, then he said, "I will not see Colonel Morris. What you tell me only confirms my opinion that we must fight this question. If he and his witnesses adhere to the story you repeat, on oath, I shall then have some tangible ground upon which to stand with Miss Blake. If they do not—and, personally, I feel satisfied no one who told such a tale could stand the test of cross-examination—we shall then have defeated the hidden enemy who, as I believe, lurks behind all this. Miss Blake is right in what she said to you: Robert Elmsdale must have had many a good hater. Whether he ever inspired that different sort of dislike which leads a man to carry on a war in secret, and try to injure this opponent's family after death, I have no means of knowing. But we must test the matter now, Patterson, and I think you had better call upon Colonel Morris and tell him so."

This service, however, to Mr. Craven's intense astonishment, I utterly declined.

I told him—respectfully, of course: under no possible conditions of life could I have spoken other than respectfully to a master I loved so well—that if a message were to be delivered viva voce from our office, it could not be so delivered by me.

I mentioned the fact that I felt no desire to be kicked downstairs. I declared that I should consider it an unseemly thing for me to engage in personal conflict with a gentleman of Colonel Morris's years and social position, and, as a final argument, I stated solemnly that I believed no number of interviews would change the opinions of our late tenant or induce him to alter his determination.

"He says he will fight," I remarked, as a finish to my speech, "and I am confident he will till he drops."

"Well, well," said Mr. Craven, "I suppose he must do so then; but meantime it is all very hard upon me."

And, indeed, so it proved; what with Miss Blake, who, of course, required frequent advances to sustain her strength during the approaching ordeal; what with policemen, who could not "undertake to be always a-watching River Hall"; what with watchmen, who kept their vigils in the nearest public-house as long as it was open, and then peacefully returned home to sleep; what with possible tenants, who came to us imagining the place was to let, and whom we referred to Colonel Morris, who dismissed them, each and all, with a tale which disenchanted them with the "desirable residence"—it was all exceeding hard upon Mr. Craven and his clerks till the quarter turned when we could take action about the matter.

Before the new year was well commenced, we were in the heat of the battle. We had written to Colonel Morris, applying for one quarter's rent of River Hall. A disreputable blackguard of a solicitor would have served him with a writ; but we were eminently respectable: not at the bidding of her most gracious Majesty, whose name we invoked on many and many of our papers, would Mr. Craven have dispensed with the preliminary letter; and I feel bound to say I follow in his footsteps in that respect.

To this notice, Colonel Morris replied, referring us to his solicitors.

We wrote to them, eliciting a reply to the effect that they would receive service of a writ. We served that writ, and then, as Colonel Morris intended to fight, instructed counsel.

Meanwhile the "Uninhabited House," and the furniture it contained, was, as Mr. Taylor tersely expressed the matter, "Going to the devil."

We could not help that, however—war was put upon us, and go to war we felt we must.

Which was all extremely hard upon Mr. Craven. To my knowledge, he had already, in three months, advanced thirty pounds to Miss Blake, besides allowing her to get into his debt for counsel's fees, and costs out of pocket, and cab hire, and Heaven knows what besides—with a problematical result also. Colonel Morris' solicitors were sparing no expenses to crush us. Clearly they, in a blessed vision, beheld an enormous bill, paid without difficulty or question. Fifty guineas here or there did not signify to their client, whilst to us—well, really, let a lawyer be as kind and disinterested as he will, fifty guineas disbursed upon the suit of an utterly insolvent, or persistently insolvent, client means something eminently disagreeable to him.

Nevertheless, we were all heartily glad to know the day of war was come. Body and soul, we all went in for Miss Blake, and Helena, and the "Uninhabited House." Even Mr. Taylor relented, and was to be seen rushing about with papers in hand relating to the impending suit of Blake v. Morris.

"She is a blank, blank woman," he remarked to me; "but still the case is interesting. I don't think ghosts have ever before come into court in my experience."

And we were all of the same mind. We girt up our loins for the fight. Each of us, I think, on the strength of her celebrity, lent Miss Blake a few shillings, and one or two of our number franked her to luncheon.

She patronized us all, I know, and said she should like to tell our mothers they had reason to be proud of their sons. And then came a dreadfully solemn morning, when we went to Westminster and championed Miss Blake.

Never in our memory of the lady had she appeared to such advantage as when we met her in Edward the Confessor's Hall. She looked a little paler than usual, and we felt her general get-up was a credit to our establishment. She wore an immense fur tippet, which, though then of an obsolete fashion, made her look like a three-per-cent. annuitant going to receive her dividends. Her throat was covered with a fine white lawn handkerchief; her dress was mercifully long enough to conceal her boots; her bonnet was perfectly straight, and the strings tied by some one who understood that bows should be pulled out and otherwise fancifully manipulated. As she carried a muff as large as a big drum, she had conceived the happy idea of dispensing altogether with gloves, and I saw that one of the fingers she gave me to shake was adorned with a diamond ring.

"Miss Elmsdale's," whispered Taylor to me. "It belonged to her mother."

Hearing which, I understood Helena had superintended her aunt's toilet.

"Did you ever see Miss Elmsdale?" I inquired of our manager.

"Not for years," was the answer. "She bade fair to be pretty."

"Why does not Miss Blake bring her out with her sometimes?" I asked.

"I believe she is expecting the Queen to give her assent to her marrying the Prince of Wales," explained Taylor, "and she does not wish her to appear much in public until after the wedding."

The court was crammed. Somehow it had got into the papers— probably through Colonel Morris' gossips at the club—that ours was likely to prove a very interesting case, and though the morning was damp and wretched, ladies and gentlemen had turned out into the fog and drizzle, as ladies and gentlemen will when there seems the least chance of a new sensation being provided for them.

Further, there were lots of reporters.

"It will be in every paper throughout the kingdom," groaned Taylor. "We had better by far have left the Colonel alone."

That had always been my opinion, but I only said, "Well, it is of no use looking back now."

I glanced at Mr. Craven, and saw he was ill at ease. We had considerable faith in ourselves, our case, and our counsel; but, then, we could not be blind to the fact that Colonel Morris' counsel were men very much better known than our men—that a cloud of witnesses, thirsting to avenge themselves for the rent we had compelled them to pay for an uninhabitable house, were hovering about the court—(had we not seen and recognized them in the Hall?)—that, in fact, there were two very distinct sides to the question, one represented by Colonel Morris and his party, and the other by Miss Blake and ourselves.

Of course our case lay in a nutshell. We had let the place, and Colonel Morris had agreed to take it. Colonel Morris now wanted to be rid of his bargain, and we were determined to keep him to it. Colonel Morris said the house was haunted, and that no one could live in it. We said the house was not haunted, and that anybody could live in it; that River Hall was "in every respect suited for the residence of a family of position"—see advertisements in Times and Morning Post.

Now, if the reader will kindly consider the matter, it must be an extremely difficult thing to prove, in a court of law, that a house, by reason solely of being haunted, is unsuitable for the residence of a gentleman of position.

Smells, bad drainage, impure water, unhealthiness of situation, dampness, the absence of advantages mentioned, the presence of small game—more odious to tenants of furnished houses than ground game to farmers—all these things had, we knew, been made pretexts for repudiation of contracts, and often successfully, but we could find no precedent for ghosts being held as just pleas upon which to relinquish a tenancy; and we made sure of a favourable verdict accordingly.

To this day, I believe that our hopes would have been justified by the result, had some demon of mischief not put it into the head of Taylor—who had the management of the case—that it would be a good thing to get Miss Blake into the witness-box.

"She will amuse the jury," he said, "and juries have always a kindly feeling for any person who can amuse them."

Which was all very well, and might be very true in a general way, but Miss Blake proved the exception to his rule.

Of course she amused the jury, in fact, she amused everyone. To get her to give a straightforward answer to any question was simply impossible.

Over and over again the judge explained to her that "yes" or "no" would be amply sufficient; but all in vain. She launched out at large in reply to our counsel, who, nevertheless, when he sat down, had gained his point.

Miss Blake declared upon oath she had never seen anything worse than herself at River Hall, and did not believe anybody else ever had.

She had never been there during Colonel Morris' tenancy, or she must certainly have seen something worse than a ghost, a man ready and anxious to "rob the orphan," and she was going to add the "widow" when peals of laughter stopped her utterance. Miss Blake had no faith in ghosts resident at River Hall, and if anybody was playing tricks about the house, she should have thought a "fighting gentleman by profession" capable of getting rid of them.

"Unless he was afraid," added Miss Blake, with withering irony.

Then up rose the opposition counsel, who approached her in an easy, conversational manner.

"And so you do not believe in ghosts, Miss Blake?" he began.

"Indeed and I don't," she answered.

"But if we have not ghosts, what is to become of the literature of your country?" he inquired.

"I don't know what you mean, by talking about my country," said Miss Blake, who was always proclaiming her nationality, and quarrelling with those who discovered it without such proclamation.

"I mean," he explained, "that all the fanciful legends and beautiful stories for which Ireland is celebrated have their origin in the supernatural. There are, for instance, several old families who have their traditional banshee."

"For that matter, we have one ourselves," agreed Miss Blake, with conscious pride.

At this junction our counsel interposed with a suggestion that there was no insinuation about any banshee residing at River Hall.

"No, the question is about a ghost, and I am coming to that. Different countries have different usages. In Ireland, as Miss Blake admits, there exists a very ladylike spirit, who announces the coming death of any member of certain families. In England, we have ghosts, who appear after the death of some members of some families. Now, Miss Blake, I want you to exercise your memory. Do you remember a night in the November after Mr. Elmsdale's death?"

"I remember many nights in many months that I passed broken-hearted in that house," she answered, composedly; but she grew very pale; and feeling there was something unexpected behind both question and answer, our counsel looked at us, and we looked back at him, dismayed.

"Your niece, being nervous, slept in the same room as that occupied by you?" continued the learned gentleman.

"She did," said Miss Blake. Her answer was short enough, and direct enough, at last.

"Now, on the particular November night to which I refer, do you recollect being awakened by Miss Elmsdale?"

"She wakened me many a time," answered Miss Blake, and I noticed that she looked away from her questioner, and towards the gallery.

"Exactly so; but on one especial night she woke you, saying, her father was walking along the passage; that she knew his step, and that she heard his keys strike against the wall?"

"Yes, I remember that," said Miss Blake, with suspicious alacrity. "She kept me up till daybreak. She was always thinking about him, poor child."

"Very natural indeed," commented our adversary. "And you told her not to be foolish, I daresay, and very probably tried to reassure her by saying one of the servants must have passed; and no doubt, being a lady possessed of energy and courage, you opened your bedroom door, and looked up and down the corridor?"

"Certainly I did," agreed Miss Blake.

"And saw nothing—and no one?"

"I saw nothing."

"And then, possibly, in order to convince Miss Elmsdale of the full extent of her delusion, you lit a candle, and went downstairs."

"Of course—why wouldn't I?" said Miss Blake, defiantly.

"Why not, indeed?" repeated the learned gentleman, pensively. "Why not?—Miss Blake being brave as she is witty. Well, you went downstairs, and, as was the admirable custom of the house—a custom worthy of all commendation—you found the doors opening from the hall bolted and locked?"

55

"I did."

"And no sign of a human being about?"

"Except myself," supplemented Miss Blake.

"And rather wishing to find that some human being besides yourself was about, you retraced your steps, and visited the servants' apartments?"

"You might have been with me," said Miss Blake, with an angry sneer.

"I wish I had," he answered. "I can never sufficiently deplore the fact of my absence. And you found the servants asleep?"

"Well, they seemed asleep," said the lady; "but that does not prove that they were so."

"Doubtless," he agreed. "Nevertheless, so far as you could judge, none of them looked as if they had been wandering up and down the corridors?"

"I could not judge one way or another," said Miss Blake: "for the tricks of English servants, it is impossible for anyone to be up to."

"Still, it did not occur to you at the time that any of them was feigning slumber?"

"I can't say it did. You see, I am naturally unsuspicious," explained Miss Blake, naively.

"Precisely so. And thus it happened that you were unable to confute Miss Elmsdale's fancy?"

"I told her she must have been dreaming," retorted Miss Blake. "People who wake all of a sudden often confound dreams with realities."

"And people who are not in the habit of awaking suddenly often do the same thing," agreed her questioner; "and so, Miss Blake, we will pass out of dreamland, and into daylight—or rather foglight. Do you recollect a particularly foggy day, when your niece, hearing a favourite dog moaning piteously, opened the door of the room where her father died, in order to let it out?"

Miss Blake set her lips tight, and looked up at the gallery. There was a little stir in that part of the court, a shuffling of feet, and suppressed whispering. In vain the crier shouted, "Silence! silence, there!" The bustle continued for about a minute, and then all became quiet again. A policeman stated "a female had fainted," and our curiosity being satisfied, we all with

56

one accord turned towards our learned friend, who, one hand under his gown, holding it back, and the other raised to emphasise his question, had stood in this picturesque attitude during the time occupied in carrying the female out, as if done in stone.

"Miss Blake, will you kindly answer my question?" he said, when order once again reigned in court.

"You're worse than a heathen," remarked the lady, irrelevantly.

"I am sorry you do not like me," he replied, "for I admire you very much; but my imperfections are beside the matter in point. What I want you to tell us is, did Miss Elmsdale open that door?"

"She did—the creature, she did," was the answer; "her heart was always tender to dumb brutes."

"I have no doubt the young lady's heart was everything it ought to be," was the reply; "and for that reason, though she had an intense repugnance to enter the room, she opened the door to let the dog out."

"She said so: I was not there," answered Miss Blake.

Whereupon ensued a brisk skirmish between counsel as to whether Miss Blake could give evidence about a matter of mere hearsay. And after they had fought for ten minutes over the legal bone, our adversary said he would put the question differently, which he did, thus:

"You were sitting in the dining-room, when you were startled by hearing a piercing shriek."

"I heard a screech—you can call it what you like," said Miss Blake, feeling an utter contempt for English phraseology.

"I stand corrected; thank you, Miss Blake. You heard a screech, in short, and you hurried across the hall, and found Miss Elmsdale in a fainting condition, on the floor of the library. Was that so?"

"She often fainted: she is all nairves," explained poor Miss Blake.

"No doubt. And when she regained consciousness, she entreated to be taken out of that dreadful room."

"She never liked the room after her father's death: it was natural, poor child."

"Quite natural. And so you took her into the dining-room, and there,

57

curled upon the hearthrug, fast asleep, was the little dog she fancied she heard whining in the library."

"Yes, he had been away for two or three days, and came home hungry and sleepy."

"Exactly. And you have, therefore, no reason to believe he was shamming slumber."

"I believe I am getting very tired of your questions and cross-questions," she said, irritably.

"Now, what a pity!" remarked her tormentor; "for I could never tire of your answers. At all events, Miss Elmsdale could not have heard him whining in the library—so called."

"She might have heard some other dog," said Miss Blake.

"As a matter of fact, however, she stated to you there was no dog in the room."

"She did. But I don't think she knew whether there was or not."

"In any case, she did not see a dog; you did not see one; and the servants did not."

"I did not," replied Miss Blake; "as to the servants, I would not believe them on their oath."

"Hush! hush! Miss Blake," entreated our opponent. "I am afraid you must not be quite so frank. Now to return to business. When Miss Elmsdale recovered consciousness, which she did in that very comfortable easy-chair in the dining-room—what did she tell you?"

"Do you think I am going to repeat her half-silly words?" demanded Miss Blake, angrily. "Poor dear, she was out of her mind half the time, after her father's death."

"No doubt; but still, I must just ask you to tell us what passed. Was it anything like this? Did she say, 'I have seen my father. He was coming out of the strong-room when I lifted my head after looking for Juan, and he was wringing his hands, and seemed in some terrible distress'?"

"God forgive them that told you her words," remarked Miss Blake; "but she did say just those, and I hope they'll do you and her as played eavesdropper all the good I wish."

58

"Really, Miss Blake," interposed the judge.

"I have no more questions to ask, my lord," said Colonel Morris' counsel, serenely triumphant. "Miss Blake can go down now."

And Miss Blake did go down; and Taylor whispered in my ear:

"She had done for us."

WE AGREE TO COMPROMISE

Colonel Morris' side of the case was now to be heard, and heads were bending eagerly forward to catch each word of wisdom that should fall from the lips of Serjeant Playfire, when I felt a hand, cold as ice, laid on mine, and turning, beheld Miss Blake at my elbow.

She was as white as the nature of her complexion would permit, and her voice shook as she whispered:

"Take me away from this place, will you?"

I cleared a way for her out of the court, and when we reached Westminster Hall, seeing how upset she seemed, asked if I could get anything for her—"a glass of water, or wine," I suggested, in my extremity.

"Neither water nor wine will mend a broken heart," she answered, solemnly; "and mine has been broken in there"—with a nod she indicated the court we had just left.

Not remembering at the moment an approved recipe for the cure of such a fracture, I was cudgelling my brains to think of some form of reply not likely to give offence, when, to my unspeakable relief, Mr. Craven came up to where we stood.

"I will take charge of Miss Blake now, Patterson," he said, gravely— very gravely; and accepting this as an intimation that he desired my absence, I was turning away, when I heard Miss Blake say:

"Where is she—the creature? What have they done with her at all?"

"I have sent her home," was Mr. Craven's reply. "How could you be so foolish as to mislead me as you have done?"

"Come," thought I, smelling the battle afar off, "we shall soon have Craven v. Blake tried privately in our office." I knew Mr. Craven pretty well, and understood he would not readily forgive Miss Blake for having kept Miss Helena's experiences a secret from him.

Over and over I had heard Miss Blake state there was not a thing really against the house, and that Helena, poor dear, only hated the place because she had there lost her father.

"Not much of a loss either, if she could be brought to think so," finished Miss Blake, sometimes.

Consequently, to Mr. Craven, as well as to all the rest of those connected with the firm, the facts elicited by Serjeant Playfire were new as unwelcome.

If the daughter of the house dreamed dreams and beheld visions, why should strangers be denied a like privilege? If Miss Elmsdale believed her father could not rest in his grave, how were we to compel belief as to calm repose on the part of yearly tenants?

"Playfire has been pitching into us pretty strong," remarked Taylor, when I at length elbowed my way back to where our manager sat. "Where is Mr. Craven?"

"I left him with Miss Blake."

"It is just as well he has not heard all the civil remarks Playfire made about our connection with the business. Hush! he is going to call his witnesses. No, the court is about to adjourn for luncheon."

Once again I went out into Westminster Hall, and was sauntering idly up and down over its stones when Mr. Craven joined me.

"A bad business this, Patterson," he remarked.

"We shall never get another tenant for that house," I answered.

"Certainly no tenant will ever again be got through me," he said, irritably; and then Taylor came to him, all in a hurry, and explaining he was wanted, carried him away.

"They are going to compromise," I thought, and followed slowly in the direction taken by my principal.

How I knew they were thinking of anything of the kind, I cannot say, but intuitively I understood the course events were taking.

Our counsel had mentally decided that, although the jury might feel inclined to uphold contracts and to repudiate ghosts, still, it would be impossible for them to overlook the fact that Colonel Morris had rented the place in utter ignorance of its antecedents, and that we had, so far, taken a perhaps undue advantage of him; moreover, the gallant officer had witnesses in court able to prove, and desirous of proving, that we had over and over again compromised matters with dissatisfied tenants, and cancelled agreements, not once or twice, but many, times; further, on no single occasion had Miss Blake and her niece ever slept a single night in the uninhabited house from the day when they left it; no matter how scarce of money they chanced to be, they went into lodgings rather than reside at River Hall. This was beyond dispute and Miss Blake's evidence supplied the reason for conduct so extraordinary.

For some reason the house was uninhabitable. The very owners could not live in it; and yet—so in imagination we heard Serjeant Playfire declaim—"The lady from whom the TRUTH had that day been reluctantly wrung had the audacity to insist that delicate women and tender children should continue to inhabit a dwelling over which a CURSE seemed brooding—a dwelling where the dead were always striving for mastery with the living; or else pay Miss Blake a sum of money which should enable her and the daughter of the suicide to live in ease and luxury on the profits of DECEPTION."

And looking at the matter candidly, our counsel did not believe the jury could return a verdict. He felt satisfied, he said, there was not a landlord in the box, that they were all tenants, who would consider the three months' rent paid over and above the actual occupation rent, ample, and more than ample, remuneration.

On the other hand, Serjeant Playfire, whose experience of juries was large, and calculated to make him feel some contempt for the judgment of "twelve honest men" in any case from pocket-picking to manslaughter, had a prevision that, when the judge had explained to Mr. Foreman and gentlemen of the jury, the nature of a contract, and told them supernatural appearances, however disagreeable, were not recognized in law as a sufficient cause for breaking an agreement, a verdict would be found for Miss Blake.

"There must be one landlord amongst them," he considered; "and if there is, he will wind the rest round his finger. Besides, they will take the side of the women, naturally; and Miss Blake made them laugh, and the way she spoke of her niece touched them; while, as for the Colonel, he won't like cross-examination, and I can see my learned friend means to make him

62

appear ridiculous. Enough has been done for honour—let us think of safety."

"For my part," said Colonel Morris, when the question was referred to him, "I am not a vindictive man, nor, I hope, an ungenerous foe; I do not like to be victimized, and I have vindicated my principles. The victory was mine in fact, if not in law, when that old Irishwoman's confession was wrung out of her. So, therefore, gentlemen, settle the matter as you please— I shall be satisfied."

And all the time he was inwardly praying some arrangement might be come to. He was brave enough in his own way, but it is one thing to go into battle, and another to stand legal fire without the chance of sending a single bullet in return. Ridicule is the vulnerable spot in the heel of many a modern Achilles; and while the rest of the court was "convulsed with laughter" over Miss Blake's cross-examination, the gallant Colonel felt himself alternately turning hot and cold when he thought that through even such an ordeal he might have to pass. And, accordingly, to cut short this part of my story, amongst them the lawyers agreed to compromise the matter thus—

Colonel Morris to give Miss Blake a third quarter's rent—in other words, fifty pounds more, and each side to pay its own costs.

When this decision was finally arrived at, Mr. Craven's face was a study. Full well he knew on whom would fall the costs of one side. He saw in prophetic vision the fifty pounds passing out of his hands into those of Miss Blake, but no revelation was vouchsafed on the subject of loans unpaid, of costs out of pocket, or costs at all. After we left court he employed himself, I fancy, for the remainder of the afternoon in making mental calculations of how much poorer a man Mrs. Elmsdale's memory, and the Uninhabited House had left him; and, upon the whole, the arithmetical problem could not have proved satisfactory when solved.

The judge complimented everyone upon the compromise effected. It was honourable in every way, and creditable to all parties concerned, but the jury evidently were somewhat dissatisfied at the turn affairs had taken, while the witnesses were like to rend Colonel Morris asunder.

"They had come, at great inconvenience to themselves, to expose the tactics of that Blake woman and her solicitor," so they said; "and they thought the affair ought not to have been hushed up."

As for the audience, they murmured openly. They received the statement that the case was over, with groans, hisses, and other marks of disapproval, and we heard comments on the matter uttered by disappointed spectators all the way up Parliament Street, till we arrived at that point where we left the main thoroughfare, in order to strike across to Buckingham Street.

There—where Pepys once lived—we betook ourselves to our books and papers, with a sense of unusual depression in the atmosphere. It was a gray, dull, cheerless afternoon, and more than one of us, looking out at the mud bank, which, at low water, then occupied the space now laid out as gardens, wondered how River Hall, desolate, tenantless, uninhabited, looked under that sullen sky, with the murky river flowing onward, day and night, day and night, leaving, unheeding, an unsolved mystery on its banks.

For a week we saw nothing of Miss Blake, but at the end of that time, in consequence of a somewhat imperative summons from Mr. Craven, she called at the office late one afternoon. We comprehended she had selected that, for her, unusual time of day for a visit, hoping our principal might have left ere she arrived; but in this hope she was disappointed: Mr. Craven was in, at leisure, and anxious to see her.

I shall never forget that interview. Miss Blake arrived about five o'clock, when it was quite dark out of doors, and when, in all our offices except Mr. Craven's, the gas was flaring away triumphantly. In his apartment he kept the light always subdued, but between the fire and the lamp there was plenty of light to see that Miss Blake looked ill and depressed, and that Mr. Craven had assumed a peculiar expression, which, to those who knew him best, implied he had made up his mind to pursue a particular course of action, and meant to adhere to his determination.

"You wanted to see me," said our client, breaking the ice.

"Yes; I wanted to tell you that our connection with the River Hall property must be considered at an end."

"Well, well, that is the way of men, I suppose—in England."

64

"I do not think any man, whether in England or Ireland, could have done more for a client than I have tried to do for you, Miss Blake," was the offended answer.

"I am sure I have never found fault with you," remarked Miss Blake, deprecatingly.

"And I do not think," continued Mr. Craven, unheeding her remark, "any lawyer ever met with a worse return for all his trouble than I have received from you."

"Dear, dear," said Miss Blake, with comic disbelief in her tone, "that is very bad."

"There are two classes of men who ought to be treated with entire confidence," persisted Mr. Craven, "lawyers and doctors. It is as foolish to keep back anything from one as from another."

"I daresay," argued Miss Blake; "but we are not all wise alike, you know."

"No," remarked my principal, who was indeed no match for the lady, "or you would never have allowed me to take your case into court in ignorance of Helena having seen her father."

"Come, come," retorted Miss Blake; "you do not mean to say you believe she ever did see her father since he was buried, and had the stone-work put all right and neat again, about him? And, indeed, it went to my heart to have a man who had fallen into such bad ways laid in the same grave with my dear sister, but I thought it would be unchristian—"

"We need not go over all that ground once more, surely," interrupted Mr. Craven. "I have heard your opinions concerning Mr. Elmsdale frequently expressed ere now. That which I never did hear, however, until it proved too late, was the fact of Helena having fancied she saw her father after his death."

"And what good would it have done you, if I had repeated all the child's foolish notions?"

"This, that I should not have tried to let a house believed by the owner herself to be uninhabitable."

"And so you would have kept us without bread to put in our mouths, or

65

a roof over our heads."

"I should have asked you to do at first what I must ask you to do at last. If you decline to sell the place, or let it unfurnished, on a long lease, to some one willing to take it, spite of its bad character, I must say the house will never again be let through my instrumentality, and I must beg you to advertise River Hall yourself, or place it in the hands of an agent."

"Do you mean to say, William Craven," asked Miss Blake, solemnly, "that you believe that house to be haunted?"

"I do not," he answered. "I do not believe in ghosts, but I believe the place has somehow got a bad name—perhaps through Helena's fancies, and that people imagine it is haunted, and get frightened probably at sight of their own shadows. Come, Miss Blake, I see a way out of this difficulty; you go and take up your abode at River Hall for six months, and at the end of that time the evil charm will be broken."

"And Helena dead," she observed.

"You need not take Helena with you."

"Nor anybody else, I suppose you mean," she remarked. "Thank you, Mr. Craven; but though my life is none too happy, I should like to die a natural death, and God only knows whether those who have been peeping and spying about the place might not murder me in my bed, if I ever went to bed in the house; that is—"

"Then, in a word, you do believe the place is haunted."

"I do nothing of the kind," she answered, angrily; "but though I have courage enough, thank Heaven, I should not like to stay all alone in any house, and I know there is not a servant in England would stay there with me, unless she meant to take my life. But I tell you what, William Craven, there are lots of poor creatures in the world even poorer than we are—tutors and starved curates, and the like. Get one of them to stay at the Hall till he finds out where the trick is, and I won't mind saying he shall have fifty pounds down for his pains; that is, I mean, of course, when he has discovered the secret of all these strange lights, and suchlike."

And feeling she had by this proposition struck Mr. Craven under the fifth rib, Miss Blake rose to depart.

"You will kindly think over what I have said," observed Mr. Craven.

"I'll do that if you will kindly think over what I have said," she retorted, with the utmost composure; and then, after a curt good-evening, she passed through the door I held open, nodding to me, as though she would have remarked, "I'm more than a match for your master still, young man."

"What a woman that is!" exclaimed Mr. Craven, as I resumed my seat.

"Do you think she really means what she says about the fifty pounds?" I inquired.

"I do not know," he answered, "but I know I would cheerfully pay that sum to anyone who could unravel the mystery of River Hall."

"Are you in earnest, sir?" I asked, in some surprise.

"Certainly I am," he replied.

"Then let me go and stay at River Hall," I said. "I will undertake to run the ghost to earth for half the money."

MY OWN STORY

It is necessary now that I should tell the readers something about my own antecedents.

Aware of how uninteresting the subject must prove, I shall make that something as short as possible.

Already it will have been clearly understood, both from my own hints, and from Miss Blake's far from reticent remarks on my position, that I was a clerk at a salary in Mr. Craven's office.

But this had not always been the case. When I went first to Buckingham Street, I was duly articled to Mr. Craven, and my mother and sister, who were of aspiring dispositions, lamented that my choice of a profession had fallen on law rather than soldiering.

They would have been proud of a young fellow in uniform; but they did not feel at all elated at the idea of being so closely connected with a "musty attorney."

As for my father, he told me to make my own choice, and found the money to enable me to do so. He was an easy-going soul, who was in the miserable position of having a sufficient income to live on without exerting either mind or body; and yet whose income was insufficient to enable him to have superior hobbies, or to gratify any particular taste. We resided in the country, and belonged to the middle class of comfortable, well-to-do English people. In our way, we were somewhat exclusive as to our associates—and as the Hall and Castle residents were, in their way, exclusive also, we lived almost out of society.

Indeed, we were very intimate with only one family in our neighbourhood; and I think it was the example of the son of that house which first induced me to think of leading a different existence from that in which my father had grown as green and mossy as a felled tree.

Ned Munro, the eldest hope of a proud but reduced stock, elected to study for the medical profession.

"The life here," he remarked, vaguely indicating the distant houses occupied by our respective sires, "may suit the old folks, but it does not suit me." And he went out into the wilderness of the world.

After his departure I found that the life at home did not suit me either, and so I followed his lead, and went, duly articled, to Mr. Craven, of Buckingham Street, Strand. Mr. Craven and my father were old friends. To this hour I thank Heaven for giving my father such a friend.

After I had been for a considerable time with Mr. Craven, there came a dreadful day, when tidings arrived that my father was ruined, and my immediate presence required at home. What followed was that which is usual enough in all such cases, with this difference—the loss of his fortune killed my father.

From what I have seen since, I believe when he took to his bed and quietly gave up living altogether, he did the wisest and best thing possible under the circumstances. Dear, simple, kindly old man, I cannot fancy how his feeble nature might have endured the years which followed; filled by my mother and sister with lamentations, though we knew no actual want— thanks to Mr. Craven.

My father had been dabbling in shares, and when the natural consequence—ruin, utter ruin, came to our pretty country home, Mr. Craven returned me the money paid to him, and offered me a salary.

Think of what this kindness was, and we penniless; while all the time relations stood aloof, holding out nor hand nor purse, till they saw whether we could weather the storm without their help.

Amongst those relations chanced to be a certain Admiral Patterson, an uncle of my father. When we were well-to-do he had not disdained to visit us in our quiet home, but when poverty came he tied up his purse-strings and ignored our existence, till at length, hearing by a mere chance that I was supporting my mother and sister by my own exertions (always helped by Mr. Craven's goodness), he said, audibly, that the "young jackanapes must have more in him than he thought," and wrote to beg that I would spend my next holiday at his house.

I was anxious to accept the invitation, as a friend told me he felt certain the old gentleman would forward my views; but I did not choose to visit my relative in shabby clothes and with empty pockets; therefore, it fell out that I jumped at Miss Blake's suggestion, and closed with Mr. Craven's offer on the spot.

Half fifty—twenty-five—pounds would replenish my wardrobe, pay my travelling expenses, and leave me with money in my pocket, as well.

I told Mr. Craven all this in a breath. When I had done so he laughed, and said:

"You have worked hard, Patterson. Here is ten pounds. Go and see your uncle; but leave River Hall alone."

Then, almost with tears, I entreated him not to baulk my purpose. If I could rid River Hall of its ghost, I would take money from him, not otherwise. I told him I had set my heart on unravelling the mystery attached to that place, and I could have told him another mystery at the same time, had shame not tied my tongue. I was in love—for the first time in my life—hopelessly, senselessly, with a face of which I thought all day and dreamed all night, that had made itself in a moment part and parcel of my story, thus:

I had been at Kentish Town to see one of our clients, and having finished my business, walked on as far as Camden Town, intending to take an omnibus which might set me down somewhere near Chancery Lane.

Whilst standing at the top of College Street, under shelter of my umbrella, a drizzling rain falling and rendering the pavement dirty and slippery, I noticed a young lady waiting to cross the road—a young lady with, to my mind, the sweetest, fairest, most lovable face on which my eyes had ever rested. I could look at her without causing annoyance, because she was so completely occupied in watching lumbering vans, fast carts, crawling cabs, and various other vehicles, which chanced at that moment to be crowding the thoroughfare, that she had no leisure to bestow even a glance on any pedestrian.

A governess, I decided: for her dress, though neat, and even elegant, was by no means costly; moreover, there was an expression of settled melancholy about her features, and further, she carried a roll, which looked like music, in her hand. In less time than it has taken me to write this paragraph, I had settled all about her to my own satisfaction.

Father bankrupt. Mother delicate. Young brothers and sisters, probably, all crying aloud for the pittance she was able to earn by giving lessons at so much an hour.

She had not been long at her present occupation, I felt satisfied, for she was evidently unaccustomed to being out in the streets alone on a wet day.

I would have offered to see her across the road, but for two reasons: one, because I felt shy about proffering my services; the other, because I was exceedingly doubtful whether I might not give offence by speaking.

After the fashion of so many of her sex, she made about half a dozen false starts, advancing as some friendly cabby made signs for her to venture the passage, retreating as she caught sight of some coming vehicle still yards distant.

At last, imagining the way clear, she made a sudden rush, and had just got well off the curb, when a mail phaeton turned the corner, and in one second she was down in the middle of the road, and I struggling with the horses and swearing at the driver, who, in his turn, very heartily anathematized me.

I do not remember all I said to the portly, well-fed, swaggering cockney upstart; but there was so much in it uncomplimentary to himself and his driving, that the crowd already assembled cheered, as all crowds will cheer profane and personal language; and he was glad enough to gather up his reins and touch his horses, and trot off, without having first gone through the ceremony of asking whether the girl he had so nearly driven over was living or dead.

Meantime she had been carried into the nearest shop, whither I followed her.

I do not know why all the people standing about imagined me to be her brother, but they certainly did so, and, under that impression, made way for me to enter the parlour behind the shop, where I found my poor beauty sitting, faint and frightened and draggled, whilst the woman of the house was trying to wipe the mud off her dress, and endeavouring to persuade her to swallow some wine-and-water.

As I entered, she lifted her eyes to mine, and said, "Thank you, sir. I trust you have not got hurt yourself," so frankly and so sweetly that the

71

small amount of heart her face had left me passed into her keeping at once.

"Are you much hurt?" I replied by asking.

"My arm is, a little," she answered. "If I could only get home! Oh! I wish I were at home."

I went out and fetched a cab, and assisted her into it. Then I asked her where the man should drive, and she gave me the name of the street which Miss Blake, when in England, honoured by making her abode. Miss Blake's number was 110. My charmer's number was 15. Having obtained this information, I closed the cab-door, and taking my seat beside the driver, we rattled off in the direction of Brunswick Square.

Arrived at the house, I helped her—when, in answer to my knock, an elderly woman appeared, to ask my business—into the narrow hall of a dreary house. Oh! how my heart ached when I beheld her surroundings! She did not bid me good-bye; but asking me into the parlour, went, as I understood, to get money to pay the cabman.

Seizing my opportunity, I told the woman, who still stood near the door, that I was in a hurry, and leaving the house, bade the driver take me to the top of Chancery Lane.

On the next Sunday I watched No. 15, till I beheld my lady-fair come forth, veiled, furred, dressed all in her dainty best, prayer-book in hand, going alone to St. Pancras Church—not the old, but the new—whither I followed her.

By some freak of fortune, the verger put me into the same pew as that in which he had just placed her.

When she saw me her face flushed crimson, and then she gave a little smile of recognition.

I fear I did not much heed the service on that particular Sunday; but I still felt shy, so shy that, after I had held the door open for her to pass out, I allowed others to come between us, and did not dare to follow and ask how she was.

During the course of the next week came Miss Blake and Mr. Craven's remark about the fifty pounds; and within four-and-twenty hours something still more astounding occurred—a visit from Miss Blake and her niece, who wanted "a good talking-to"—so Miss Blake stated.

It was a dull, foggy day, and when my eyes rested on the younger lady, I drew back closer into my accustomed corner, frightened and amazed.

"You were in such a passion yesterday," began Miss Blake, coming into the office, dragging her blushing niece after her, "that you put it out of my head to tell you three things—one, that we have moved from our old lodgings; the next, that I have not a penny to go on with; and the third, that Helena here has gone out of her mind. She won't have River Hall let again, if you please. She intends to go out as a governess—what do you think of that?—and nothing I can say makes any impression upon her. I should have thought she had had enough of governessing the first day she went out to give a lesson: she got herself run over and nearly killed; was brought back in a cab by some gentleman, who had the decency to take the cab away again: for how we should have paid the fare, I don't know, I am sure. So I have just brought her to you to know if her mother's old friend thinks it is a right thing for Kathleen Elmsdale's daughter to put herself under the feet of a parcel of ignorant, purse-proud snobs?"

Mr. Craven looked at the girl kindly. "My dear," he said, "I think, I believe, there will be no necessity for you to do anything of that kind. We have found a person—have we not, Patterson?—willing to devote himself to solving the River Hall mystery. So, for the present at all events, Helena—"

He paused, for Helena had risen from her seat and crossed the room to where I sat.

"Aunt, aunt," she said, "this is the gentleman who stopped the horses," and before I could speak a word she held my hand in hers, and was thanking me once again with her beautiful eyes.

Miss Blake turned and glared upon me. "Oh! it was you, was it?" she said, ungraciously. "Well, it is just what I might have expected, and me hoping all the time it was a lord or a baronet, at the least."

We all laughed—even Miss Elmsdale laughed at this frank confession; but when the ladies were gone, Mr. Craven, looking at me pityingly, remarked:

"This is a most unfortunate business, Patterson. I hope—I do hope, you

73

will not be so foolish as to fall in love with Miss Elmsdale."

To which I made no reply. The evil, if evil it were, was done. I had fallen in love with Miss Blake's niece ere those words of wisdom dropped from my employer's lips.

MY FIRST NIGHT AT RIVER HALL

It was with a feeling of depression for which I could in no way account that, one cold evening, towards the end of February, I left Buckingham Street and wended my way to the Uninhabited House. I had been eager to engage in the enterprise; first, for the sake of the fifty pounds reward; and secondly, and much more, for the sake of Helena Elmsdale. I had tormented Mr. Craven until he gave a reluctant consent to my desire. I had brooded over the matter until I became eager to commence my investigations, as a young soldier may be to face the enemy; and yet, when the evening came, and darkness with it; when I set my back to the more crowded thoroughfares, and found myself plodding along a lonely suburban road, with a keen wind lashing my face, and a suspicion of rain at intervals wetting my cheeks, I confess I had no feeling of enjoyment in my self-imposed task.

After all, talking about a haunted house in broad daylight to one's fellow-clerks, in a large London office, is a very different thing from taking up one's residence in the same house, all alone, on a bleak winter's night, with never a soul within shouting distance. I had made up my mind to go through with the matter, and no amount of mental depression, no wintry blasts, no cheerless roads, no desolate goal, should daunt me; but still I did not like the adventure, and at every step I felt I liked it less.

Before leaving town I had fortified my inner man with a good dinner and some excellent wine, but by the time I reached River Hall I might have fasted for a week, so faint and spiritless did I feel.

"Come, this will never do," I thought, as I turned the key in the door, and crossed the threshold of the Uninhabited House. "I must not begin with being chicken-hearted, or I may as well give up the investigation at once."

The fires I had caused to be kindled in the morning, though almost out by the time I reached River Hall, had diffused a grateful warmth throughout the house; and when I put a match to the paper and wood laid ready in the grate of the room I meant to occupy, and lit the gas, in the hall, on the landing, and in my sleeping-apartment, I began to think things did not look so cheerless, after all.

The seals which, for precaution's sake, I had placed on the various locks, remained intact. I looked to the fastenings of the hall-door, examined the screws by which the bolts were attached to the wood, and having satisfied myself that everything of that kind was secure, went up to my room, where the fire was now crackling and blazing famously, put the kettle on the hob, drew a chair up close to the hearth, exchanged my boots for slippers, lit a pipe, pulled out my law-books, and began to read.

How long I had read, I cannot say; the kettle on the hob was boiling, at any rate, and the coals had burned themselves into a red-hot mass of glowing cinders, when my attention was attracted—or rather, I should say, distracted—by the sound of tapping outside the window-pane. First I listened, and read on, then I laid down my book and listened more attentively. It was exactly the noise which a person would make tapping upon glass with one finger.

The wind had risen almost to a tempest, but, in the interval between each blast, I could hear the tapping as distinctly as if it had been inside my own skull—tap, tap, imperatively; tap, tap, tap, impatiently; and when I rose to approach the casement, it seemed as if three more fingers had joined in the summons, and were rapping for bare life.

"They have begun betimes," I thought; and taking my revolver in one hand, with the other I opened the shutters, and put aside the blind.

As I did so, it seemed as if some dark body occupied one side of the sash, while the tapping continued as madly as before.

It is as well to confess at once that I was for the moment frightened. Subsequently I saw many wonderful sights, and had some terrible experiences in the Uninhabited House; but I can honestly say, no sight or experience so completely cowed me for the time being, as that dull blackness to which I could assign no shape, that spirit-like rapping of fleshless fingers, which seemed to increase in vehemence as I obeyed its summons.

Doctors say it is not possible for the heart to stand still and a human being live, and, as I am not a doctor, I do not like to contradict their dogma, otherwise I could positively declare my heart did cease beating as I listened, looking out into the night with the shadow of that darkness projecting itself upon my mind, to the impatient tapping, which was now distinctly audible even above the raging of the storm.

How I gathered sufficient courage to do it, I cannot tell; but I put my face close to the glass, thus shutting out the gas and fire-light, and saw that the dark object which alarmed me was a mass of ivy the wind had detached from the wall, and that the invisible fingers were young branches straying from the main body of the plant, which, tossed by the air-king, kept striking the window incessantly, now one, now two, now three, tap, tap, tap; tap, tap; tap, tap; and sometimes, after a long silence, all together, tap-p-p, like the sound of clamming bells.

I stood for a minute or two, listening to the noise, so as to satisfy myself as to its cause, then I laid down the revolver, took out my pocket-knife, and opened the window. As I did so, a tremendous blast swept into the room, extinguishing the gas, causing the glowing coals to turn, for a moment, black on one side and to fiercest blaze on the other, scattering the dust lying on the hearth over the carpet, and dashing the ivy-sprays against my face with a force which caused my cheeks to smart and tingle long afterwards.

Taking my revenge, I cut them as far back as I could, and then, without closing the window, and keeping my breath as well as I could, I looked out across the garden over the Thames, away to the opposite bank, where a few lights glimmered at long intervals. "An eerie, lonely place for a fellow to be in all by himself," I continued; "and yet, if the rest of the ghosts, bodiless or clothed with flesh, which frequent this house prove to be as readily laid as those ivy-twigs, I shall earn my money—and—my—thanks, easily enough."

So considering, I relit the gas, replenished the fire, refilled my pipe, reseated myself by the hearth, and with feet stretched out towards the genial blaze, attempted to resume my reading.

All in vain: I could not fix my attention on the page; I could not connect one sentence with another. When my mind ought to have concentrated its energies upon Justice That, and Vice-Chancellor This, and Lord Somebody Else, I felt it wandering away, trying to fit together all the odds and ends of evidence worthy or unworthy concerning the Uninhabited House. Which really was, as we had always stated, a good house, a remarkably good house, well furnished, suitable in every respect, &c.

Had I been a "family of respectability," or a gentleman of position, with a large number of servants, a nice wife, and a few children sprinkled about the domestic picture, I doubt not I should have enjoyed the contemplation of that glowing fire, and rejoiced in the idea of finding myself located in so desirable a residence, within an easy distance of the West End; but, as matters stood, I felt anything rather than elated.

In that large house there was no human inmate save myself, and I had an attack of nervousness upon me for which I found it impossible to account. Here was I, at length, under the very roof where my mistress had passed all her childish days, bound to solve the mystery which was making such havoc with her young life, permitted to essay a task, the accomplishment of which should cover me with glory, and perhaps restore peace and happiness to her heart; and yet I was afraid. I did not hesitate to utter that word to my own soul then, any more than I hesitate to write it now for those who list to read: for I can truly say I think there are few men whose courage such an adventure would not try were they to attempt it; and I am sure, had any one of those to whom I tell this story been half as much afraid as I, he would have left River Hall there and then, and allowed the ghosts said to be resident, to haunt it undisturbed for evermore.

If I could only have kept memory from running here and there in quest of evidence pro and con the house being haunted, I should have fared better: but I could not do this.

Let me try as I would to give my attention to those legal studies that ought to have engrossed my attention, I could not succeed in doing so: my thoughts, without any volition on my part, kept continually on the move; now with Miss Blake in Buckingham Street, again with Colonel Morris on the river walk, once more with Miss Elmsdale in the library; and went constantly flitting hither and thither, recalling the experiences of a frightened lad, or the terror of an ignorant woman; yet withal I had a feeling that in some way memory was playing me false, as if, when ostentatiously bringing out all her stores for me to make or mar as I could, she had really hidden away, in one of her remotest corners, some link, great or little as the case might be, but still, whether great or little, necessary to connect the unsatisfactory narratives together.

Till late in the night I sat trying to piece my puzzle together, but without success. There was a flaw in the story, a missing point in it, somewhere, I felt certain. I often imagined I was about to touch it, when, heigh! presto! it eluded my grasp.

"The whole affair will resolve itself into ivy-boughs," I finally, if not truthfully, decided. "I am satisfied it is all—ivy," and I went to bed.

Now, whether it was that I had thought too much of the ghostly narratives associated with River Hall, the storminess of the night, the fact of sleeping in a strange room, or the strength of a tumbler of brandy-and-water, in which brandy took an undue lead, I cannot tell; but during the morning hours I dreamed a dream which filled me with an unspeakable horror, from which I awoke struggling for breath, bathed in a cold perspiration, and with a dread upon me such as I never felt in any waking moment of my life.

I dreamt I was lying asleep in the room I actually occupied, when I was aroused from a profound slumber by the noise produced by some one tapping at the window-pane. On rising to ascertain the cause of this summons, I saw Colonel Morris standing outside and beckoning me to join him. With that disregard of space, time, distance, and attire which obtains in dreams, I at once stepped out into the garden. It was a pitch-dark night, and bitterly cold, and I shivered, I know, as I heard the sullen flow of the river, and listened to the moaning of the wind among the trees.

We walked on for some minutes in silence, then my companion asked me if I felt afraid, or if I would go on with him.

"I will go where you go," I answered.

Then suddenly he disappeared, and Playfire, who had been his counsel at the time of the trial, took my hand and led me onwards.

We passed through a doorway, and, still in darkness, utter darkness, began to descend some steps. We went down—down—hundreds of steps as it seemed to me, and in my sleep, I still remembered the old idea of its being

79

unlucky to dream of going downstairs. But at length we came to the bottom, and then began winding along interminable passages, now so narrow only one could walk abreast, and again so low that we had to stoop our heads in order to avoid striking the roof.

After we had been walking along these for hours, as time reckons in such cases, we commenced ascending flight after flight of steep stone-steps. I laboured after Playfire till my limbs ached and grew weary, till, scarcely able to drag my feet from stair to stair, I entreated him to stop; but he only laughed and held on his course the more rapidly, while I, hurrying after, often stumbled and recovered myself, then stumbled again and lay prone.

The night air blew cold and chill upon me as I crawled out into an unaccustomed place and felt my way over heaps of uneven earth and stones that obstructed my progress in every direction. I called out for Playfire, but the wind alone answered me; I shouted for Colonel Morris; I entreated some one to tell me where I was; and in answer there was a dead and terrible silence. The wind died away; not a breath of air disturbed the heavy stillness which had fallen so suddenly around me. Instead of the veil of merciful blackness which had hidden everything hitherto from view, a gray light spread slowly over the objects around, revealing a burial-ground, with an old church standing in the midst—a burial-ground where grew rank nettles and coarse, tall grass; where brambles trailed over the graves, and weeds and decay consorted with the dead.

Moved by some impulse which I could not resist, I still held on my course, over mounds of earth, between rows of headstones, till I reached the other side of the church, under the shadow of which yawned an open pit. To the bottom of it I peered, and there beheld an empty coffin; the lid was laid against the side of the grave, and on a headstone, displaced from its upright position, sat the late occupant of the grave, looking at me with wistful, eager eyes. A stream of light from within the church fell across that one empty grave, that one dead watcher.

"So you have come at last," he said; and then the spell was broken, and I would have fled, but that, holding me with his left hand, he pointed with his right away to a shadowy distance, where the gray sky merged into

80

deepest black.

I strained my eyes to discover the object he strove to indicate, but I failed to do so. I could just discern something flitting away into the darkness, but I could give it no shape or substance.

"Look—look!" the dead man said, rising, in his excitement, and clutching me more firmly with his clay-cold fingers.

I tried to fly, but I could not; my feet were chained to the spot. I fought to rid myself of the clasp of the skeleton hand, and then we fell together over the edge of the pit, and I awoke.

A TEMPORARY PEACE

It was scarcely light when I jumped out of bed, and murmuring, "Thank God it was only a dream," dressed myself with all speed, and flinging open the window, looked out on a calm morning after the previous night's storm.

Muddily and angrily the Thames rolled onward to the sea. On the opposite side of the river I could see stretches of green, with here and there a house dotting the banks.

A fleet of barges lay waiting the turn of the tide to proceed to their destination. The voices of the men shouting to each other, and blaspheming for no particular reason, came quite clear and distinct over the water. The garden was strewed with twigs and branches blown off the trees during the night; amongst them the sprigs of ivy I had myself cut off.

An hour and a scene not calculated to encourage superstitious fancies, it may be, but still not likely to enliven any man's spirits—a quiet, dull, gray, listless, dispiriting morning, and, being country-bred, I felt its influence.

"I will walk into town, and ask Ned Munro to give me some breakfast," I thought, and found comfort in the idea.

Ned Munro was a doctor, but not a struggling doctor. He was not rich, but he "made enough for a beginner": so he said. He worked hard for little pay; "but I mean some day to have high pay, and take the world easy," he explained. He was blessed with great hopes and good courage; he had high spirits, and a splendid constitution. He neither starved himself nor his friends; his landlady "loved him as her son"; and there were several good-looking girls who were very fond of him, not as a brother.

But Ned had no notion of marrying, yet awhile. "Time enough for that," he told me once, "when I can furnish a good house, and set up a brougham, and choose my patients, and have a few hundreds lying idle in the bank."

Meantime, as no one of these items had yet been realized, he lived in lodgings, ate toasted haddocks with his morning coffee, and smoked and read novels far into the night.

Yes, I could go and breakfast with Munro. Just then it occurred to me that the gas I had left lighted when I went to bed was out; that the door I had left locked was open.

Straight downstairs I went. The gas in the hall was out, and every door I had myself closed and locked the previous morning stood ajar, with the seal, however, remaining intact.

I had borne as much as I could: my nerves were utterly unhinged. Snatching my hat and coat, I left the house, and fled, rather than walked, towards London.

With every step I took towards town came renewed courage; and when I reached Ned's lodgings, I felt ashamed of my pusillanimity.

"I have been sleep-walking, that is what it is," I decided. "I have opened the doors and turned off the gas myself, and been frightened at the work of my own hands. I will ask Munro what is the best thing to insure a quiet night."

Which I did accordingly, receiving for answer—

"Keep a quiet mind."

"Yes, but if one cannot keep a quiet mind; if one is anxious and excited, and——"

"In love," he finished, as I hesitated.

"Well, no; I did not mean that," I said; "though, of course, that might enter into the case also. Suppose one is uneasy about a certain amount of money, for instance?"

"Are you?" he asked, ignoring the general suggestiveness of my remark.

"Well, yes; I want to make some if I can."

"Don't want, then," he advised. "Take my word for it, no amount of money is worth the loss of a night's rest; and you have been tossing about all night, I can see. Come, Patterson, if it's forgery or embezzlement, out with it, man, and I will help you if I am able."

"If it were either one or the other, I should go to Mr. Craven," I answered, laughing.

"Then it must be love," remarked my host; "and you will want to take me into your confidence some day. The old story, I suppose: beautiful girl, stern parents, wealthy suitor, poor lover. I wonder if we could interest her in a case of small-pox. If she took it badly, you might have a chance; but I have a presentiment that she has been vaccinated."

"Ned," was my protest, "I shall certainly fling a plate at your head."

"All right, if you think the exertion would do you good," he answered. "Give me your hand, Patterson"; and before I knew what he wanted with it, he had his fingers on my wrist.

"Look here, old fellow," he said; "you will be laid up, if you don't take care of yourself. I thought so when you came in, and I am sure of it now. What have you been doing?"

"Nothing wrong, Munro," I answered, smiling in spite of myself. "I have not been picking, or stealing, or abducting any young woman, or courting my neighbour's wife; but I am worried and perplexed. When I sleep I have dreadful dreams—horrible dreams," I added, shuddering.

"Can you tell me what is worrying and perplexing you?" he asked, kindly, after a moment's thought.

"Not yet, Ned," I answered; "though I expect I shall have to tell you soon. Give me something to make me sleep quietly: that is all I want now."

"Can't you go out of town?" he inquired.

"I do not want to go out of town," I answered.

"I will make you up something to strengthen your nerves," he said, after a pause; "but if you are not better—well, before the end of the week, take my advice, and run down to Brighton over Sunday. Now, you ought to give me a guinea for that," he added, laughing. "I assure you, all the gold-headed cane, all the wonderful chronometer doctors who pocket thousands per annum at the West End, could make no more of your case than I have done."

"I am sure they could not," I said, gratefully; "and when I have the guinea to spare, be sure I shall not forget your fee."

Whether it was owing to his medicine, or his advice, or his cheery, health-giving manner, I have no idea; but that night, when I walked towards the Uninhabited House, I felt a different being.

On my way I called at a small corn-chandler's, and bought a quartern of flour done up in a thin and utterly insufficient bag. I told the man the wrapper would not bear its contents, and he said he could not help that.

I asked him if he had no stronger bags. He answered that he had, but he could not afford to give them away.

I laid down twopence extra, and inquired if that would cover the expense of a sheet of brown paper.

Ashamed, he turned aside and produced a substantial bag, into which he put the flour in its envelope of curling-tissue.

I thanked him, and pushed the twopence across the counter. With a grunt, he thrust the money back. I said good-night, leaving current coin of the realm to the amount indicated behind me.

Through the night be shouted, "Hi! sir, you've forgotten your change."

Through the night I shouted back, "Give your next customer its value in civility."

All of which did me good. Squabbling with flesh and blood is not a bad preliminary to entering a ghost-haunted house.

Once again I was at River Hall. Looking up at its cheerless portal, I was amazed at first to see the outside lamp flaring away in the darkness. Then I remembered that all the other gas being out, of course this, which I had not turned off, would blaze more brightly.

Purposely I had left my return till rather late. I had gone to one of the theatres, and remained until a third through the principal piece. Then I called at a supper-room, had half a dozen oysters and some stout; after which, like a giant refreshed, I wended my way westward.

Utterly false would it be for me to say I liked the idea of entering the Uninhabited House; but still, I meant to do it, and I did.

No law-books for me that night; no seductive fire; no shining lights all over the house. Like a householder of twenty years' standing, I struck a match, and turned the gas on to a single hall-lamp. I did not trouble myself even about shutting the doors opening into the hall; I only strewed flour copiously over the marble pavement, and on the first flight of stairs, and then, by the servant's passages, crept into the upper story, and so to bed.

That night I slept dreamlessly. I awoke in broad daylight, wondering why I had not been called sooner, and then remembered there was no one to call, and that if I required hot water, I must boil it for myself.

With that light heart which comes after a good night's rest, I put on some part of my clothing, and was commencing to descend the principal staircase, when my proceedings of the previous night flashed across my mind; and pausing, I looked down into the hall. No sign of a foot on the flour. The white powder lay there innocent of human pressure as the untrodden snow; and yet, and yet, was I dreaming—could I have been drunk without my own knowledge, before I went to bed? The gas was ablaze in the hall and on the staircase, and every door left open over-night was close shut.

Curiously enough, at that moment fear fell from me like a garment which has served its turn, and in the strength of my manhood, I felt able to face anything the Uninhabited House might have to show.

Over the latter part of that week, as being utterly unimportant in its events or consequences, I pass rapidly, only saying that, when Saturday came, I followed Munro's advice, and ran down to Brighton, under the idea that by so doing I should thoroughly strengthen myself for the next five days' ordeal. But the idea was a mistaken one. The Uninhabited House took its ticket for Brighton by the same express; it got into the compartment with me; it sat beside me at dinner; it hob-nobbed to me over my own wine; uninvited it came out to walk with me; and when I stood still, listening to the band, it stood still too. It went with me to the pier, and when the wind blew, as the wind did, it said, "We were quite as well off on the Thames."

When I woke, through the night, it seemed to shout, "Are you any better off here?" And when I went to church the next day it crept close up to me in the pew, and said, "Come, now, it is all very well to say you are a Christian; but if you were really one you would not be afraid of the place you and I wot of."

Finally, I was so goaded and maddened that I shook my fist at the sea, and started off by the evening train for the Uninhabited House.

This time I travelled alone. The Uninhabited House preceded me.

There, in its old position, looking gloomy and mysterious in the shadows of night, I found it on my return to town; and, as if tired of playing tricks with one who had become indifferent to their vagaries, all the doors remained precisely as I had left them; and if there were ghosts in the house that night, they did not interfere with me or the chamber I occupied.

Next morning, while I was dressing, a most remarkable thing occurred; a thing for which I was in no wise prepared. Spirits, and sights and sounds supposed appropriate to spirithood, I had expected; but for a modest knock at the front door I was not prepared.

When, after hurriedly completing my toilet, I undrew the bolts and undid the chain, and opened the door wide, there came rushing into the house a keen easterly wind, behind which I beheld a sad-faced woman, dressed in black, who dropped me a curtsey, and said:

"If you please, sir—I suppose you are the gentleman?"

Now, I could make nothing out of this, so I asked her to be good enough to explain.

Then it all came out: "Did I want a person to char?"

This was remarkable—very. Her question amazed me to such an extent that I had to ask her in, and request her to seat herself on one of the hall chairs, and go upstairs myself, and think the matter over before I answered her.

It had been so impressed upon me that no one in the neighbourhood would come near River Hall, that I should as soon have thought of Victoria by the grace of God paying me a friendly visit, as of being waited on by a charwoman.

I went downstairs again.

At sight of me my new acquaintance rose from her seat, and began curling up the corner of her apron.

"Do you know," I said, "that this house bears the reputation of being haunted?"

"I have heard people say it is, sir," she answered.

"And do you know that servants will not stay in it—that tenants will not occupy it?"

"I have heard so, sir," she answered once again.

"Then what do you mean by offering to come?" I inquired.

She looked up into my face, and I saw the tears come softly stealing into her eyes, and her mouth began to pucker, ere, drooping her head, she replied:

"Sir, just three months ago, come the twentieth, I was a happy woman. I had a good husband and a tidy home. There was not a lady in the land I would have changed places with. But that night, my man, coming home in a fog, fell into the river and was drowned. It was a week before they found him, and all the time—while I had been hoping to hear his step every minute in the day—I was a widow."

"Poor soul!" I said, involuntarily.

"Well, sir, when a man goes, all goes. I have done my best, but still I have not been able to feed my children—his children—properly, and the sight of their poor pinched faces breaks my heart, it do, sir," and she burst out sobbing.

"And so, I suppose," I remarked, "you thought you would face this house rather than poverty?"

"Yes, sir. I heard the neighbours talking about this place, and you, sir, and I made up my mind to come and ask if I mightn't tidy up things a bit for you, sir. I was a servant, sir, before I married, and I'd be so thankful."

Well, to cut the affair shorter for the reader than I was able to do for myself, I gave her half a crown, and told her I would think over her proposal, and let her hear from me—which I did. I told her she might come for a couple of hours each morning, and a couple each evening, and she could bring one of the children with her if she thought she was likely to find the place lonely.

I would not let her come in the day-time, because, in the quest I had set myself, it was needful I should feel assured no person could have an opportunity of elaborating any scheme for frightening me, on the premises.

"Real ghosts," said I to Mr. Craven, "I do not mind; but the physical agencies which may produce ghosts, I would rather avoid." Acting on which principle I always remained in the house while Mrs. Stott—my charwoman was so named—cleaned, and cooked, and boiled, and put things straight.

No one can imagine what a revolution this woman effected in my ways and habits, and in the ways and habits of the Uninhabited House.

Tradesmen called for orders. The butcher's boy came whistling down the lane to deliver the rump-steak or mutton-chop I had decided on for dinner; the greengrocer delivered his vegetables; the cheesemonger took solemn affidavit concerning the freshness of his stale eggs and the superior quality of a curious article which he called country butter, and declared came from a particular dairy famed for the excellence of its produce; the milkman's yahoo sounded cheerfully in the morning hours; and the letter-box was filled with cards from all sorts and descriptions of people—from laundresses to wine merchants, from gardeners to undertakers.

The doors now never shut nor opened of their own accord. A great peace seemed to have settled over River Hall.

It was all too peaceful, in fact. I had gone to the place to hunt a ghost, and not even the ghost of a ghost seemed inclined to reveal itself to me.

THE WATCHER IS WATCHED

I have never been able exactly to satisfy my own mind as to the precise period during my occupation of the Uninhabited House when it occurred to me that I was being watched. Hazily I must have had some consciousness of the fact long before I began seriously to entertain the idea.

I felt, even when I was walking through London, that I was being often kept in sight by some person. I had that vague notion of a stranger being interested in my movements which it is so impossible to define to a friend, and which one is chary of seriously discussing with oneself. Frequently, when the corner of a street was reached, I found myself involuntarily turning to look back; and, prompted by instinct, I suppose, for there was no reason about the matter, I varied my route to and from the Uninhabited House, as much as the nature of the roads permitted. Further, I ceased to be punctual as to my hours of business, sometimes arriving at the office late, and, if Mr. Craven had anything for me to do Cityward, returning direct from thence to River Hall without touching Buckingham Street.

By this time February had drawn to a close, and better weather might therefore have been expected; instead of which, one evening as I paced westward, snow began to fall, and continued coming down till somewhere about midnight.

Next morning Mrs. Stott drew my attention to certain footmarks on the walks, and beneath the library and drawing-room windows—the footmarks, evidently, of a man whose feet were not a pair. With the keenest interest, I examined these traces of a human pursuer. Clearly the footprints had been made by only one person, and that person deformed in some way. Not merely was the right foot-track different from that of the left, but the way in which its owner put it to the ground must have been different also. The one mark was clear and distinct, cut out in the snow with a firm tread, while the other left a little broken bank at its right edge, and scarcely any impression of the heel.

"Slightly lame," I decided. "Eases his right foot, and has his boots made to order."

"It is very odd," I remarked aloud to Mrs. Stott.

"That it is, sir," she answered; adding, "I hope to gracious none of them mobsmen are going to come burglaring here!" "Pooh!" I replied; "there is nothing for them to steal, except chairs and tables, and I don't think one man could carry many of them away."

The whole of that day I found my thoughts reverting to those foot-marks in the snow. What purpose anyone proposed to serve by prowling about River Hall I could not imagine. Before taking up my residence in the Uninhabited House, I had a theory that some malicious person or persons was trying to keep the place unoccupied—nay, further, imagination suggested the idea that, owing to its proximity to the river, Mr. Elmsdale's Hall might have taken the fancy of a gang of smugglers, who had provided for themselves means of ingress and egress unknown to the outside world. But all notions of this kind now seemed preposterous.

Slowly, but surely, the conviction had been gaining upon me that, let the mystery of River Hall be what it would, no ordinary explanation could account for the phenomena which it had presented to tenant after tenant; and my own experiences in the house, slight though they were, tended to satisfy me there was something beyond malice or interest at work about the place.

The very peace vouchsafed to me seemed another element of mystery, since it would certainly have been natural for any evil-disposed person to inaugurate a series of ghostly spectacles for the benefit of an investigator like myself; and yet, somehow, the absence of supernatural appearances, and the presence of that shadowy human being who thought it worth while to track my movements, and who had at last left tangible proof of his reality behind him in the snow, linked themselves together in my mind.

"If there is really anyone watching me," I finally decided, "there must be a deeper mystery attached to River Hall than has yet been suspected. Now, the first thing is to make sure that some one is watching me, and the next to guard against danger from him."

In the course of the day, I made a, for me, curious purchase. In a little shop, situated in a back street, I bought half a dozen reels of black sewing-cotton.

This cotton, on my return home, I attached to the trellis-work outside the drawing-room window, and wound across the walk and round such trees and shrubs as grew in positions convenient for my purpose.

"If these threads are broken to-morrow morning, I shall know I have a flesh-and-blood foe to encounter," I thought.

Next morning I found all the threads fastened across the walks leading round by the library and drawing-room snapped in two.

It was, then, flesh and blood I had come out to fight, and I decided that night to keep watch.

As usual, I went up to my bedroom, and, after keeping the gas burning for about the time I ordinarily spent in undressing, put out the light, softly turned the handle of the door, stole, still silently, along the passage, and so into a large apartment with windows which overlooked both the library and drawing-room.

It was here, I knew, that Miss Elmsdale must have heard her father walking past the door, and I am obliged to confess that, as I stepped across the room, a nervous chill seemed for the moment to take my courage captive.

If any reader will consider the matter, mine was not an enviable position. Alone in a desolate house, reputed to be haunted, watching for some one who had sufficient interest in the place to watch it and me closely.

It was still early—not later than half-past ten. I had concluded to keep my vigil until after midnight, and tried to while away the time with thoughts foreign to the matter in hand.

All in vain, however. Let me force what subject I pleased upon my mind, it reverted persistently to Mr. Elmsdale and the circumstances of his death.

"Why did he commit suicide?" I speculated. "If he had lost money, was that any reason why he should shoot himself?"

People had done so, I was aware; and people, probably, would continue to do so; but not hard-headed, hard-hearted men, such as Robert Elmsdale was reputed to have been. He was not so old that the achievement of a second success should have seemed impossible. His credit was good, his actual position unsuspected. River Hall, unhaunted, was not a bad property, and in those days he could have sold it advantageously.

I could not understand the motive of his suicide, unless, indeed, he was mad or drunk at the time. And then I began to wonder whether anything about his life had come out on the inquest—anything concerning habits, associates, and connections. Had there been any other undercurrent, besides betting, in his life brought out in evidence, which might help me to a solution of the mystery?

"I will ask Mr. Craven to-morrow," I thought, "whether he has a copy of the Times, containing a report of the inquest. Perhaps—"

What possibility I was about to suggest to my own mind I shall never now know, for at that moment there flamed out upon the garden a broad, strong flame of light—a flame which came so swiftly and suddenly, that a man, creeping along the River Walk, had not time to step out of its influence before I had caught full sight of him. There was not much to see, however. A man about the middle height, muffled in a cloak, wearing a cap, the peak of which was drawn down over his forehead: that was all I could discern, ere, cowering back from the light, he stole away into the darkness.

Had I yielded to my first impulse, I should have rushed after him in pursuit; but an instant's reflection told me how worse than futile such a wild-goose chase must prove. Cunning must be met with cunning, watching with watching.

If I could discover who he was, I should have taken the first step towards solving the mystery of River Hall; but I should never do so by putting him on his guard. The immediate business lying at that moment to my hand was to discover whence came the flare of light which, streaming across the walk, had revealed the intruder's presence to me. For that business I can truthfully say I felt little inclination.

Nevertheless, it had to be undertaken. So, walking downstairs, I unlocked and opened the library-door, and found, as I anticipated, the room in utter darkness. I examined the fastenings of the shutters—they were secure as I had left them; I looked into the strong-room—not even a rat lay concealed there; I turned the cocks of the gas lights—but no gas whistled

93

through the pipes, for the service to the library was separate from that of the rest of the house, and capable of being shut off at pleasure. I, mindful of the lights said to have been seen emanating from that room, had taken away the key from the internal tap, so that gas could not be used without my knowledge or the possession of a second key. Therefore, as I have said, it was no surprise to me to find the library in darkness. Nor could I say the fact of the light flaring, apparently, from a closely-shut-up room surprised me either. For a long time I had been expecting to see this phenomenon: now, when I did see it, I involuntarily connected the light, the apartment, and the stranger together.

For he was no ghost. Ghosts do not leave footmarks behind them in the snow. Ghosts do not break threads of cotton. It was a man I had seen in the garden, and it was my business to trace out the connection between him and the appearances at River Hall.

Thinking thus, I left the library, extinguished the candle by the aid of which I had made the investigations stated above, and after lowering the gaslight I always kept burning in the hall, began ascending the broad, handsome staircase, when I was met by the figure of a man descending the steps. I say advisedly, the figure; because, to all external appearance, he was as much a living man as myself.

And yet I knew the thing which came towards me was not flesh and blood. Knew it when I stood still, too much stupefied to feel afraid. Knew it, as the figure descended swiftly, noiselessly. Knew it, as, for one instant, we were side by side. Knew it, when I put out my hand to stop its progress, and my hand, encountering nothing, passed through the phantom as through air. Knew, it, when I saw the figure pass through the door I had just locked, and which opened to admit the ghostly visitor—opened wide, and then closed again, without the help of mortal hand.

After that I knew nothing more till I came to my senses again and found myself half lying, half sitting on the staircase, with my head resting against the banisters. I had fainted; but if any man thinks I saw in a vision what I have described, let him wait till he reaches the end of this story before expressing too positive an opinion about the matter.

94

How I passed the remainder of that night, I could scarcely tell. Towards morning, however, I fell asleep, and it was quite late when I awoke: so late, in fact, that Mrs. Stott had rung for admittance before I was out of bed.

That morning two curious things occurred: one, the postman brought a letter for the late owner of River Hall, and dropped it in the box; another, Mrs. Stott asked me if I would allow her and two of the children to take up their residence at the Uninhabited House. She could not manage to pay her rent, she explained, and some kind friends had offered to maintain the elder children if she could keep the two youngest.

"And I thought, sir, seeing how many spare rooms there are here, and the furniture wanting cleaning, and the windows opening when the sun is out, that perhaps you would not object to my staying here altogether. I should not want any more wages, sir, and I would do my best to give satisfaction."

For about five minutes I considered this proposition, made to me whilst sitting at breakfast, and decided in favour of granting her request. I felt satisfied she was not in league with the person or persons engaged in watching my movements; it would be well to have some one in care of the premises during my absence, and it would clearly be to her interest to keep her place at River Hall, if possible.

Accordingly, when she brought in my boots, I told her she could remove at once if she liked.

"Only remember one thing, Mrs. Stott," I said. "If you find any ghosts in the dark corners, you must not come to me with any complaints."

"I sleep sound, sir," she answered, "and I don't think any ghosts will trouble me in the daytime. So thank you, sir; I will bring over a few things and stay here, if you please."

"Very good; here is the key of the back door," I answered; and in five minutes more I was trudging Londonward.

As I walked along I decided not to say anything to Mr. Craven concerning the previous night's adventures; first, because I felt reluctant to mention the apparition, and secondly, because instinct told me I should do

95

better to keep my own counsel, and confide in no one, till I had obtained some clue to the mystery of that midnight watcher.

"Now here's a very curious thing!" said Mr. Craven, after he had opened and read the letter left at River Hall that morning. "This is from a man who has evidently not heard of Mr. Elmsdale's death, and who writes to say how much he regrets having been obliged to leave England without paying his I O U held by my client. To show that, though he may have seemed dishonest, he never meant to cheat Mr. Elmsdale, he encloses a draft on London for the principal and interest of the amount due."

"Very creditable to him," I remarked. "What is the amount, sir?"

"Oh! the total is under a hundred pounds," answered Mr. Craven; "but what I meant by saying the affair seemed curious is this: amongst Mr. Elmsdale's papers there was not an I O U of any description."

"Well, that is singular," I observed; then asked, "Do you think Mr. Elmsdale had any other office besides the library at River Hall?"

"No," was the reply, "none whatever. When he gave up his offices in town, he moved every one of his papers to River Hall. He was a reserved, but not a secret man; not a man, for instance, at all likely to lead a double life of any sort."

"And yet he betted," I suggested.

"Certainly that does puzzle me," said Mr. Craven. "And it is all against my statement, for I am certain no human being, unless it might be Mr. Harringford, who knew him in business, was aware of the fact."

"And what is your theory about the absence of all-important documents?" I inquired.

"I think he must have raised money on them," answered Mr. Craven.

"Are you aware whether anyone else ever produced them?" I asked.

"I am not; I never heard of their being produced: but, then, I should not have been likely to hear." Which was very true, but very unsatisfactory. Could we succeed in tracing even one of those papers, a clue might be found to the mystery of Mr. Elmsdale's suicide.

That afternoon I repaired to the house of one of our clients, who had, I knew, a file of the Times newspapers, and asked him to allow me to look at

96

it.

I could, of course, have seen a file at many places in the city, but I preferred pursuing my investigations where no one was likely to watch the proceeding.

"Times! bless my soul, yes; only too happy to be able to oblige Mr. Craven. Walk into the study, there is a good fire, make yourself quite at home, I beg, and let me send you a glass of wine."

All of which I did, greatly to the satisfaction of the dear old gentleman.

Turning over the file for the especial year in which Mr. Elmsdale had elected to put a pistol to his head, I found at last the account of the inquest, which I copied out in shorthand, to be able to digest it more fully at leisure; and as it was growing dusk, wended my way back to Buckingham Street.

As I was walking slowly down one side of the street, I noticed a man standing within the open door of a house near Buckingham Gate.

At any other time I should not have given the fact a second thought, but life at River Hall seemed to have endowed me with the power of making mountains out of molehills, of regarding the commonest actions of my fellows with distrust and suspicion; and I was determined to know more of the gentleman who stood back in the shadow, peering out into the darkening twilight.

With this object I ran upstairs to the clerk's office, and then passed into Mr. Craven's room. He had gone, but his lamp was still burning, and I took care to move between it and the window, so as to show myself to any person who might be watching outside; then, without removing hat or top-coat, I left the room, and proceeded to Taylor's office, which I found in utter darkness. This was what I wanted; I wished to see without being seen; and across the way, standing now on the pavement, was the man I had noticed, looking up at our offices.

"All right," thought I, and running downstairs, I went out again, and walked steadily up Buckingham Street, along John Street, up Adam Street, as though en route to the Strand. Before, however, I reached that thoroughfare, I paused, hesitated, and then immediately and suddenly wheeled round and retraced my steps, meeting, as I did so, a man walking a few yards behind me and at about the same pace.

I did not slacken my speed for a moment as we came face to face; I did not turn to look back after him; I retraced my steps to the office; affected to look out some paper, and once again pursued my former route, this time without meeting or being followed by anyone, and made my way into the City, where I really had business to transact.

I could have wished for a longer and a better look at the man who honoured me so far as to feel interested in my movements; but I did not wish to arouse his suspicions.

I had scored one trick; I had met him full, and seen his face distinctly—so distinctly that I was able to feel certain I had seen it before, but where, at the moment, I could not remember.

"Never mind," I continued: "that memory will come in due time; meanwhile the ground of inquiry narrows, and the plot begins to thicken."

MISS BLAKE ONCE MORE

Upon my return to River Hall I found in the letter-box an envelope addressed to —— Patterson, Esq.

Thinking it probably contained some circular, I did not break the seal until after dinner; whereas, had I only known from whom the note came, should I not have devoured its contents before satisfying the pangs of physical hunger!

Thus ran the epistle:—

"DEAR SIR,—

"Until half an hour ago I was ignorant that you were the person who had undertaken to reside at River Hall. If you would add another obligation to that already conferred upon me, leave that terrible house at once. What I have seen in it, you know; what may happen to you, if you persist in remaining there, I tremble to think. For the sake of your widowed mother and only sister, you ought not to expose yourself to a risk which is worse than useless. I never wish to hear of River Hall being let again. Immediately I come of age, I shall sell the place; and if anything could give me happiness in this world, it would be to hear the house was razed to the ground. Pray! pray! listen to a warning, which, believe me, is not idly given, and leave a place which has already been the cause of so much misery to yours, gratefully and sincerely,

"HELENA ELMSDALE."

It is no part of this story to tell the rapture with which I gazed upon the writing of my "lady-love." Once I had heard Miss Blake remark, when Mr. Craven was remonstrating with her on her hieroglyphics, that "Halana wrote an 'unmaning hand,' like all the rest of the English," and, to tell the truth, there was nothing particularly original or characteristic about Miss Elmsdale's calligraphy.

But what did that signify to me? If she had strung pearls together, I should not have valued them one-half so much as I did the dear words which revealed her interest in me.

Over and over I read the note, at first rapturously, afterwards with a second feeling mingling with my joy. How did she know it was I who had taken up my residence at River Hall? Not a soul I knew in London, besides Mr. Craven, was aware of the fact, and he had promised faithfully to keep my secret.

Where, then, had Miss Elmsdale obtained her information? from whom had she learned that I was bent on solving the mystery of the "Uninhabited House"?

I puzzled myself over these questions till my brain grew uneasy with vain conjectures.

Let me imagine what I would—let me force my thoughts into what grooves I might—the moment the mental pressure was removed, my suspicions fluttered back to the man whose face seemed not unfamiliar.

"I am confident he wants to keep that house vacant," I decided. "Once let me discover who he is, and the mystery of the 'Uninhabited House' shall not long remain a mystery."

But then the trouble chanced to be how to find out who he was. I could not watch and be watched at the same time, and I did not wish to take anyone into my confidence, least of all a professional detective.

So far fortune had stood my friend; I had learnt something suspected by no one else, and I made up my mind to trust to the chapter of accidents for further information on the subject of my unknown friend.

When Mr. Craven and I were seated at our respective tables, I said to him:

"Could you make any excuse to send me to Miss Blake's to-day, sir?"

Mr. Craven looked up in utter amazement. "To Miss Blake's!" he repeated. "Why do you want to go there?"

"I want to see Miss Elmsdale," I answered, quietly enough, though I felt the colour rising in my face as I spoke.

"You had better put all that nonsense on one side, Patterson," he remarked. "What you have to do is to make your way in the world, and you will not do that so long as your head is running upon pretty girls. Helena

Elmsdale is a good girl; but she would no more be a suitable wife for you, than you would be a suitable husband for her. Stick to law, my lad, for the present, and leave love for those who have nothing more important to think of."

"I did not want to see Miss Elmsdale for the purpose you imply," I said, smiling at the vehemence of Mr. Craven's advice. "I only wish to ask her one question."

"What is the question?"

"From whom she learned that I was in residence at River Hall," I answered, after a moment's hesitation.

"What makes you think she is aware of that fact?" he inquired.

"I received a note from her last night, entreating me to leave the place, and intimating that some vague peril menaced me if I persisted in remaining there."

"Poor child! poor Helena!" said Mr. Craven, thoughtfully; then spreading a sheet of note-paper on his blotting-pad, and drawing his cheque-book towards him, he proceeded:

"Now remember, Patterson, I trust to your honour implicitly. You must not make love to that girl; I think a man can scarcely act more dishonourably towards a woman, than to induce her to enter into what must be, under the best circumstances, a very long engagement."

"You may trust me, sir," I answered, earnestly. "Not," I added, "that I think it would be a very easy matter to make love to anyone with Miss Blake sitting by."

Mr. Craven laughed; he could not help doing so at the idea I had suggested. Then he said, "I had a letter from Miss Blake this morning asking me for money."

"And you are going to let her have some of that hundred pounds you intended yesterday to place against her indebtedness to you," I suggested.

"That is so," he replied. "Of course, when Miss Helena comes of age, we must turn over a new leaf—we really must."

To this I made no reply. It would be a most extraordinary leaf, I considered, in which Miss Blake did not appear as debtor to my employer but it scarcely fell within my province to influence Mr. Craven's actions.

"You had better ask Miss Blake to acknowledge receipt of this," said my principal, holding up a cheque for ten pounds as he spoke. "I am afraid I have not kept the account as I ought to have done."

Which was undeniably true, seeing we had never taken a receipt from her at all, and that loans had been debited to his private account instead of to that of Miss Blake. But true as it was, I only answered that I would get her acknowledgment; and taking my hat, I walked off to Hunter Street.

Arrived there, I found, to my unspeakable joy, that Miss Blake was out, and Miss Elmsdale at home.

When I entered the shabby sitting-room where her beauty was so grievously lodged, she rose and greeted me with kindly words, and sweet smiles, and vivid blushes.

"You have come to tell me you are not going ever again to that dreadful house," she said, after the first greeting and inquiries for Miss Blake were over. "You cannot tell the horror with which the mere mention of River Hall now fills me."

"I hope it will never be mentioned to you again till I have solved the mystery attached to it," I answered.

"Then you will not do what I ask," she cried, almost despairingly.

"I cannot," was my reply. "Miss Elmsdale, you would not have a soldier turn back from the battle. I have undertaken to find out the secret attached to your old home, and, please God, I shall succeed in my endeavours."

"But you are exposing yourself to danger, to—"

"I must take my chance of that. I cannot, if I would, turn back now, and I would not if I could. But I have come to you for information. How did you know it was I who had gone to River Hall?"

The colour flamed up in her face as I put the question.

"I—I was told so," she stammered out.

"May I ask by whom?"

"No, Mr. Patterson, you may not," she replied. "A—a friend—a kind friend, informed me of the fact, and spoke of the perils to which you were

102

exposing yourself—living there all alone—all alone," she repeated. "I would not pass a night in the house again if the whole parish were there to keep me company, and what must it be to stay in that terrible, terrible place alone! You are here, perhaps, because you do not believe—because you have not seen."

"I do believe," I interrupted, "because I have seen; and yet I mean to go through with the matter to the end. Have you a likeness of your father in your possession, Miss Elmsdale?" I asked.

"I have a miniature copied from his portrait, which was of course too large to carry from place to place," she answered. "Why do you wish to know?"

"If you let me see it, I will reply to your question," I said.

Round her dear throat she wore a thin gold chain. Unfastening this, she handed to me the necklet, to which was attached a locket enamelled in black. It is no exaggeration to say, as I took this piece of personal property, my hand trembled so much that I could not open the case.

True love is always bashful, and I loved the girl, whose slender neck the chain had caressed, so madly and senselessly, if you will, that I felt as if the trinket were a living thing, a part and parcel of herself.

"Let me unfasten it," she said, unconscious that aught save awkwardness affected my manipulation of the spring. And she took the locket and handed it back to me open, wet with tears—her tears.

Judge how hard it was for me then to keep my promise to Mr. Craven and myself—how hard it was to refrain from telling her all my reasons for having ever undertaken to fight the dragon installed at River Hall.

I thank God I did refrain. Had I spoken then, had I presumed upon her sorrow and her simplicity, I should have lost something which constitutes the sweetest memory of my life.

But that is in the future of this story, and meantime I was looking at the face of her father.

I looked at it long and earnestly; then I closed the locket, softly pressing down the spring as I did so, and gave back miniature and chain into her hand.

"Well, Mr. Patterson?" she said, inquiringly.

"Can you bear what I have to tell?" I asked.

"I can, whatever it may be," she answered.

"I have seen that face at River Hall."

She threw up her arms with a gesture of despair.

"And," I went on, "I may be wrong, but I think I am destined to solve the mystery of its appearance."

She covered her eyes, and there was silence between us for a minute, when I said:

"Can you give me the name of the person who told you I was at River Hall?"

"I cannot," she repeated. "I promised not to mention it."

"He said I was in danger."

"Yes, living there all alone."

"And he wished you to warn me."

"No; he asked my aunt to do so, and she refused; and so I—I thought I would write to you without mentioning the matter to her."

"You have done me an incalculable service," I remarked, "and in return I will tell you something."

"What is that?" she asked.

"From to-night I shall not be alone in the house."

"Oh! how thankful I am!" she exclaimed; then instantly added, "Here is my aunt."

I rose as Miss Blake entered, and bowed.

"Oh! it is you, is it?" said the lady. "The girl told me some one was waiting."

Hot and swift ran the colour to my adored one's cheeks.

"Aunt," she observed, "I think you forget this gentleman comes from Mr. Craven."

"Oh, no! my dear, I don't forget Mr. Craven, or his clerks either," responded Miss Blake, as, still cloaked and bonneted, she tore open Mr. Craven's envelope.

"I am to take back an answer, I think," said I.

104

"You are, I see," she answered. "He's getting mighty particular, is William Craven. I suppose he thinks I am going to cheat him out of his paltry ten pounds. Ten pounds, indeed! and what is that, I should like to know, to us in our present straits! Why, I had more than twice ten yesterday from a man on whom we have no claim—none whatever—who, without asking, offered it in our need."

"Aunt," said Miss Elmsdale, warningly.

"If you will kindly give me your acknowledgment, Miss Blake, I should like to be getting back to Buckingham Street," I said. "Mr. Craven will wonder at my absence."

"Not a bit of it," retorted Miss Blake. "You and Mr. Craven understand each other, or I am very much mistaken; but here is the receipt, and good day to you."

I should have merely bowed my farewell, but that Miss Elmsdale stood up valiantly.

"Good-bye, Mr. Patterson," she said, holding out her dainty hand, and letting it lie in mine while she spoke. "I am very much obliged to you. I can never forget what you have done and dared in our interests."

And I went out of the room, and descended the stairs, and opened the front door, she looking graciously over the balusters the while, happy, ay, and more than happy.

What would I not have done and dared at that moment for Helena Elmsdale? Ah! ye lovers, answer!

HELP

"There has been a gentleman to look at the house, sir, this afternoon," said Mrs. Stott to me, when, wet and tired, I arrived, a few evenings after my interview with Miss Elmsdale, at River Hall.

"To look at the house!" I repeated. "Why, it is not to let."

"I know that, sir, but he brought an order from Mr. Craven's office to allow him to see over the place, and to show him all about. For a widow lady from the country, he said he wanted it. A very nice gentleman, sir; only he did ask a lot of questions, surely—"

"What sort of questions?" I inquired.

"Oh! as to why the tenants did not stop here, and if I thought there was anything queer about the place; and he asked how you liked it, and how long you were going to stay; and if you had ever seen aught strange in the house.

"He spoke about you, sir, as if he knew you quite well, and said you must be stout-hearted to come and fight the ghosts all by yourself. A mighty civil, talkative gentleman—asked me if I felt afraid of living here, and whether I had ever met any spirits walking about the stairs and passages by themselves."

"Did he leave the order you spoke of just now behind him?"

"Yes, sir. He wanted me to give it back to him; but I said I must keep it for you to see. So then he laughed, and made the remark that he supposed, if he brought the lady to see the place, I would let him in again. A pleasant-spoken gentleman, sir—gave me a shilling, though I told him I did not require it."

Meantime I was reading the order, written by Taylor, and dated two years back.

"What sort of looking man was he?" I asked.

"Well, sir, there was not anything particular about him in any way. Not a tall gentleman, not near so tall as you, sir; getting into years, but still very active and light-footed, though with something of a halt in his way of walking. I could not rightly make out what it was; nor what it was that

106

caused him to look a little crooked when you saw him from behind.

"Very lean, sir; looked as if the dinners he had eaten done him no good. Seemed as if, for all his pleasant ways, he must have seen trouble, his face was so worn-like."

"Did he say if he thought the house would suit?" I inquired.

"He said it was a very nice house, sir, and that he imagined anybody not afraid of ghosts might spend two thousand a year in it very comfortably. He said he should bring the lady to see the place, and asked me particularly if I was always at hand, in case he should come tolerably early in the morning."

"Oh!" was my comment, and I walked into the dining-room, wondering what the meaning of this new move might be; for Mrs. Stott had described, to the best of her ability, the man who stood watching our offices in London; and—good heavens!—yes, the man I had encountered in the lane leading to River Hall, when I went to the Uninhabited House, after Colonel Morris' departure.

"That is the man," thought I, "and he has some close, and deep, and secret interest in the mystery associated with this place, the origin of which I must discover."

Having arrived at this conclusion, I went to bed, for I had caught a bad cold, and was aching from head to foot, and had been sleeping ill, and hoped to secure a good night's rest.

I slept, it is true, but as for rest, I might as well, or better, have been awake. I fell from one dream into another; found myself wandering through impossible places; started in an agony of fear, and then dozed again, only to plunge into some deeper quagmire of trouble; and through all there was a vague feeling I was pursuing a person who eluded all my efforts to find him; playing a terrible game of hide-and-seek with a man who always slipped away from my touch, panting up mountains and running down declivities after one who had better wind and faster legs than I; peering out into the darkness, to catch a sight of a vague figure standing somewhere in the shadow, and looking, with the sun streaming into my eyes and blinding me, adown long white roads filled with a multitude of people, straining my sight

107

to catch a sight of the coming traveller, who yet never came.

When I awoke thoroughly, as I did long and long before daybreak, I knew I was ill. I had a bad sore throat and an oppression at my chest which made me feel as if I was breathing through a sponge. My limbs ached more than had been the case on the previous evening whilst my head felt heavier than a log of teak.

"What should I do if I were to have a bad illness in that house?" I wondered to myself, and for a few minutes I pondered over the expediency of returning home; but this idea was soon set aside.

Where could I go that the Uninhabited House would not be a haunting presence? I had tried running away from it once before, and found it more real to me in the King's Road, Brighton, than on the banks of the Thames. No!—ill or well, I would stay on; the very first night of my absence might be the night of possible explanation.

Having so decided, I dressed and proceeded to the office, remaining there, however, only long enough to write a note to Mr. Craven, saying I had a very bad cold, and begging him to excuse my attendance.

After that I turned my steps to Munro's lodgings. If it were possible to avert an illness, I had no desire to become invalided in Mr. Elmsdale's Hall.

Fortunately, Munro was at home and at dinner. "Just come in time, old fellow," he said, cheerily. "It is not one day in a dozen you would have found me here at this hour. Sit down, and have some steak. Can't eat—why, what's the matter, man? You don't mean to say you have got another nervous attack. If you have, I declare I shall lodge a complaint against you with Mr. Craven."

"I am not nervous," I answered; "but I have caught cold, and I want you to put me to rights."

"Wait till I have finished my dinner," he replied; and then he proceeded to cut himself another piece of steak—having demolished which, and seen cheese placed on the table, he said:

"Now, Harry, we'll get to business, if you please. Where is this cold you were talking about?"

I explained as well as I could, and he listened to me without

108

interruption. When I had quite finished, he said:

"Hal Patterson, you are either becoming a hypochondriac, or you are treating me to half confidences. Your cold is not worth speaking about. Go home, and get to bed, and take a basin of gruel, or a glass of something hot, after you are in bed, and your cold will be well in the morning. But there is something more than a cold the matter with you. What has come to you, to make a few rheumatic pains and a slight sore throat seem of consequence in your eyes?"

"I am afraid of being ill," I answered.

"Why are you afraid of being ill? why do you imagine you are going to be ill? why should you fall ill any more than anybody else?"

I sat silent for a minute, then I said, "Ned, if I tell you, will you promise upon your honour not to laugh at me?"

"I won't, if I can help it. I don't fancy I shall feel inclined to laugh," he replied.

"And unless I give you permission, you will not repeat what I am going to tell you to anyone?"

"That I can safely promise," he said. "Go on."

And I went on. I began at the beginning and recited all the events chronicled in the preceding pages; and he listened, asking no questions, interposing no remark.

When I ceased speaking, he rose and said he must think over the statements I had made.

"I will come and look you up to-night, Patterson," he observed. "Go home to River Hall, and keep yourself quiet. Don't mention that you feel ill. Let matters go on as usual. I will be with you about nine. I have an appointment now that I must keep."

Before nine Munro appeared, hearty, healthy, vigorous as usual.

"If this place were in Russell Square," he said, after a hasty glance round the drawing-room, "I should not mind taking a twenty-one years' lease of it at forty pounds a year, even if ghosts were included in the fixtures."

"I see you place no credence in my story," I said, a little stiffly.

109

"I place every credence in your story," was the reply. "I believe you believe it, and that is saying more than most people could say nowadays about their friends' stories if they spoke the truth."

It was of no use for me to express any further opinion upon the matter. I felt if I talked for a thousand years I should still fail to convince my listener there was anything supernatural in the appearances beheld at River Hall. It is so easy to pooh-pooh another man's tale; it is pleasant to explain every phenomenon that the speaker has never witnessed; it is so hard to credit that anything absolutely unaccountable on natural grounds has been witnessed by your dearest friend, that, knowing my only chance of keeping my temper and preventing Munro gaining a victory over me was to maintain a discreet silence, I let him talk on and strive to account for the appearances I had witnessed in his own way.

"Your acquaintance of the halting gait and high shoulder may or might have some hand in the affair," he finished. "My own opinion is he has not. The notion that you are being watched, is, if my view of the matter be correct, only a further development of the nervous excitement which has played you all sort of fantastic tricks since you came to this house. If anyone does wander through the gardens, I should set him down as a monomaniac or an intending burglar, and in any case the very best thing you can do is to pack up your traps and leave River Hall to its fate."

I did not answer; indeed, I felt too sick at heart to do so. What he said was what other people would say. If I could not evolve some clearer theory than I had yet been able to hit on, I should be compelled to leave the mystery of River Hall just as I had found it. Miss Blake had, I knew, written to Mr. Craven that the house had better be let again, as there "was no use in his keeping a clerk there in free lodgings for ever": and now came Ned Munro, with his worldly wisdom, to assure me mine was a wild-goose chase, and that the only sensible course for me to pursue was to abandon it altogether. For the first time, I felt disheartened about the business, and I suppose I showed my disappointment, for Munro, drawing his chair nearer to me, laid a friendly hand on my shoulder and said:

"Cheer up, Harry! never look so downhearted because your nervous system has been playing you false. It was a plucky thing to do, and to carry out; but you have suffered enough for honour, and I should not continue the experiment of trying how much you can suffer, were I in your shoes."

"You are very kind, Munro," I answered; "but I cannot give up. If I had all the wish in the world to leave here to-night, a will stronger than my own would bring me back here to-morrow. The place haunts me. Believe me, I suffer less from its influence, seated in this room, than when I am in the office or walking along the Strand."

"Upon the same principle, I suppose, that a murderer always carries the memory of his victim's face about with him; though he may have felt callously indifferent whilst the body was an actual presence."

"Precisely," I agreed.

"But then, my dear fellow, you are not a murderer in any sense of the word. You did not create the ghosts supposed to be resident here."

"No; but I feel bound to find out who did," I answered.

"That is, if you can, I suppose?" he suggested.

"I feel certain I shall," was the answer. "I have an idea in my mind, but it wants shape. There is a mystery, I am convinced, to solve which, only the merest hint is needed."

"There are a good many things in this world in the same position, I should say," answered Munro. "However, Patterson, we won't argue about the matter; only there is one thing upon which I am determined—after this evening, I will come and stay here every night. I can say I am going to sleep out of town. Then, if there are ghosts, we can hunt them together; if there are none, we shall rest all the better. Do you agree to that?" and he held out his hand, which I clasped in mine, with a feeling of gratitude and relief impossible to describe.

As he said, I had done enough for honour; but still I could not give up, and here was the support and help I required so urgently, ready for my need.

"I am so much obliged," I said at last.

"Pooh! nonsense!" he answered. "You would do as much or more for me any day. There, don't let us get sentimental. You must not come out, but, following the example of your gallant Colonel Morris, I will, if you please, smoke a cigar in the garden. The moon must be up by this time."

I drew back the curtains and unfastened the shutter, which offered egress to the grounds, then, having rung for Mrs. Stott to remove the supper-tray, I sat down by the fire to await Munro's return, and began musing concerning the hopelessness of my position, the gulf of poverty and prejudice and struggle that lay between Helena and myself.

I was determined to win her; but the prize seemed unattainable as the Lord Mayor's robes must have appeared to Whittington, when he stood at the foot of Highgate Hill; and, prostrated as I was by that subtle malady to which as yet Munro had given no name, the difficulties grew into mountains, the chances of success dwarfed themselves into molehills.

Whilst thus thinking vaguely, purposelessly, but still most miserably, I was aroused from reverie by the noise of a door being shut cautiously and carefully—an outer door, and yet one with the sound of which I was unacquainted.

Hurrying across the hall, I flung the hall-door wide, and looked out into the night. There was sufficient moonlight to have enabled me to discern any object moving up or down the lane, but not a creature was in sight, not a cat or dog even traversed the weird whiteness of that lonely thoroughfare.

Despite Munro's dictum, I passed out into the night air, and went down to the very banks of the Thames. There was not a boat within hail. The nearest barge lay a couple of hundred yards from the shore.

As I retraced my steps, I paused involuntarily beside the door, which led by a separate entrance to the library.

"That is the door which shut," I said to myself, pressing my hand gently along the lintel, and sweeping the hitherto unbroken cobwebs away as I did so. "If my nerves are playing me false this time, the sooner their tricks are stopped the better, for no human being opened this door, no living creature has passed through it."

Having made up my mind on which points, I re-entered the house, and walked into the drawing-room, where Munro, pale as death, stood draining a glass of neat brandy.

"What is the matter?" I cried, hurriedly. "What have you seen, what—"

"Let me alone for awhile," he interrupted, speaking in a thick, hoarse whisper; then immediately asked, "Is that the library with the windows nearest the river?"

"Yes," I answered.

"I want to go into that room," he said, still in the same tone.

"Not now," I entreated. "Sit down and compose yourself; we will go into it, if you like, before you leave."

"Now, now—this minute," he persisted. "I tell you, Patterson, I must see what is in it."

Attempting no further opposition, I lit a couple of candles, and giving one into his hand, led the way to the door of the library, which I unlocked and flung wide open.

To one particular part Munro directed his steps, casting the light from his candle on the carpet, peering around in search of something he hoped, and yet still feared, to see. Then he went to the shutters and examined the fastenings, and finding all well secured, made a sign for me to precede him out of the room. At the door he paused, and took one more look into the darkness of the apartment, after which he waited while I turned the key in the lock, accompanying me back across the hall.

When we were once more in the drawing-room, I renewed my inquiry as to what he had seen; but he bade me let him alone, and sat mopping great beads of perspiration off his forehead, till, unable to endure the mystery any longer, I said:

"Munro, whatever it may be that you have seen, tell me all, I entreat. Any certainty will be better than the possibilities I shall be conjuring up for myself."

He looked at me wearily, and then drawing his hand across his eyes, as if trying to clear his vision, he answered, with an uneasy laugh:

"It was nonsense, of course. I did not think I was so imaginative, but I declare I fancied I saw, looking through the windows of that now utterly dark room, a man lying dead on the floor."

"Did you hear a door shut?" I inquired.

"Distinctly," he answered; "and what is more, I saw a shadow flitting through the other door leading out of the library, which we found, if you remember, bolted on the inside."

"And what inference do you draw from all this?"

"Either that some one is, in a to me unintelligible way, playing a very clever game at River Hall, or else that I am mad."

"You are no more mad than other people who have lived in this house," I answered.

"I don't know how you have done it, Patterson," he went on, unheeding my remark. "I don't, upon my soul, know how you managed to stay on here. It would have driven many a fellow out of his mind. I do not like leaving you. I wish I had told my landlady I should not be back. I will, after this time; but to-night I am afraid some patient may be wanting me."

"My dear fellow," I answered, "the affair is new to you, but it is not new to me. I would rather sleep alone in the haunted house, than in a mansion filled from basement to garret, with the unsolved mystery of this place haunting me."

"I wish you had never heard of, nor seen, nor come near it," he exclaimed, bitterly; "but, however, let matters turn out as they will, I mean to stick to you, Patterson. There's my hand on it."

And he gave me his hand, which was cold as ice—cold as that of one dead.

"I am going to have some punch, Ned," I remarked. "That is, if you will stop and have some."

"All right," he answered. "Something 'hot and strong' will hurt neither of us, but you ought to have yours in bed. May I give it to you there?"

"Nonsense!" I exclaimed, and we drew our chairs close to the fire, and, under the influence of a decoction which Ned insisted upon making himself, and at making which, indeed, he was much more of an adept than I, we talked valiantly about ghosts and their doings, and about how our credit and happiness were bound up in finding out the reason why the Uninhabited House was haunted.

"Depend upon it, Hal," said Munro, putting on his coat and hat, preparatory to taking his departure, "depend upon it that unfortunate Robert

Elmsdale must have been badly cheated by some one, and sorely exercised in spirit, before he blew out his brains."

To this remark, which, remembering what he had said in the middle of the day, showed the wonderful difference that exists between theory and practice, I made no reply.

Unconsciously, almost, a theory had been forming in my own mind, but I felt much corroboration of its possibility must be obtained before I dare give it expression.

Nevertheless, it had taken such hold of me that I could not shake off the impression, which was surely, though slowly, gaining ground, even against the dictates of my better judgment.

"I will just read over the account of the inquest once again," I decided, as I bolted and barred the chain after Munro's departure; and so, by way of ending the night pleasantly, I took out the report, and studied it till two, chiming from a neighbouring church, reminded me that the fire was out, that I had a bad cold, and that I ought to have been between the blankets and asleep hours previously.

LIGHT AT LAST

N ow, whether it was owing to having gone out the evening before from a very warm room into the night air, and, afterwards, into that chilly library, or to having sat reading the report given about Mr. Elmsdale's death till I grew chilled to my very marrow, I cannot say, all I know is, that when I awoke next morning I felt very ill, and welcomed, with rejoicing of spirit, Ned Munro, who arrived about mid-day, and at once declared he had come to spend a fortnight with me in the Uninhabited House.

"I have arranged it all. Got a friend to take charge of my patients; stated that I am going to pay a visit in the country, and so forth. And now, how are you?"

I told him, very truthfully, that I did not feel at all well.

"Then you will have to get well, or else we shall never be able to fathom this business," he said. "The first thing, consequently, I shall do, is to write a prescription, and get it made up. After that, I mean to take a survey of the house and grounds."

"Do precisely what you like," I answered. "This is Liberty Hall to the living as well as to the dead," and I laid my head on the back of the easy-chair, and went off to sleep.

All that day Munro seemed to feel little need of my society. He examined every room in the house, and every square inch about the premises. He took short walks round the adjacent neighbourhood, and made, to his own satisfaction, a map of River Hall and the country and town thereunto adjoining. Then he had a great fire lighted in the library, and spent the afternoon tapping the walls, trying the floors, and trying to obtain enlightenment from the passage which led from the library direct to the door opening into the lane.

After dinner, he asked me to lend him the shorthand report I had made of the evidence given at the inquest. He made no comment upon it when he finished reading, but sat, for a few minutes, with one hand shading his eyes, and the other busily engaged in making some sort of a sketch on the back of an old letter.

"What are you doing, Munro?" I asked, at last.

"You shall see presently," he answered, without looking up, or pausing in his occupation.

At the expiration of a few minutes, he handed me over the paper, saying:

"Do you know anyone that resembles?"

I took the sketch, looked at it, and cried out incoherently in my surprise.

"Well," he went on, "who is it?"

"The man who follows me! The man I saw in this lane!"

"And what is his name?"

"That is precisely what I desire to find out," I answered. "When did you see him? How did you identify him? Why did—"

"I have something to tell you, if you will only be quiet, and let me speak," he interrupted. "It was, as you know, late last night before I left here, and for that reason, and also because I was perplexed and troubled, I walked fast—faster than even is my wont. The road was very lonely; I scarcely met a creature along the road, flooded with the moonlight. I never was out on a lovelier night; I had never, even in the country, felt I had it so entirely to myself.

"Every here and there I came within sight of the river, and it seemed, on each occasion, as though a great mirror had been put up to make every object on land—every house, every tree, bush, fern, more clearly visible than it had been before. I am coming to my story, Hal, so don't look so impatient.

"At last, as I came once again in view of the Thames, with the moon reflected in the water, and the dark arches of the bridge looking black and solemn contrasted against the silvery stream, I saw before me, a long way before me, a man whose figure stood out in relief against the white road—a man walking wearily and with evident difficulty—a man, too, slightly deformed.

"I walked on rapidly, till within about a score yards of him, then I slackened my speed, and taking care that my leisurely footsteps should be heard, overtook him by degrees, and then, when I was quite abreast, asked if

117

he could oblige me with a light.

"He looked up in my face, and said, with a forced, painful smile and studied courtesy of manner:

"'I am sorry, sir, to say that I do not smoke.'

"I do not know exactly what reply I made. I know his countenance struck me so forcibly, it was with difficulty I could utter some commonplace remark concerning the beauty of the night.

"'I do not like moonlight,' he said, and as he said it, something, a connection of ideas, or a momentary speculation, came upon me so suddenly, that once again I failed to reply coherently, but asked if he could tell me the shortest way to the Brompton Road.

"'To which end?' he inquired.

"'That nearest Hyde Park Corner,' I answered.

"As it turned out, no question could have served my purpose better.

"'I am going part of the way there,' he said, 'and will show you the nearest route—that is,' he added, 'if you can accommodate your pace to mine,' and he pointed, as he spoke, to his right foot, which evidently was causing him considerable pain.

"Now, that was something quite in my way, and by degrees I got him to tell me about the accident which had caused his slight deformity. I told him I was a doctor, and had been to see a patient, and so led him on to talk about sickness and disease, till at length he touched upon diseases of a morbid character; asking me if it were true that in some special maladies the patient was haunted by an apparition which appeared at a particular hour.

"I told him it was quite true, and that such cases were peculiarly distressing, and generally proved most difficult to cure—mentioning several well-authenticated instances, which I do not mean to detail to you, Patterson, as I know you have an aversion to anything savouring of medical shop.

"'You doctors do not believe in the actual existence of any such apparitions, of course?' he remarked, after a pause.

"I told him we did not; that we knew they had their rise and origin solely in the malady of the patient.

"'And yet,' he said, 'some ghost stories—I am not now speaking of

118

those associated with disease, are very extraordinary, unaccountable—'

"'Very extraordinary, no doubt,' I answered; 'but I should hesitate before saying unaccountable. Now, there is that River Hall place up the river. There must be some rational way of explaining the appearances in that house, though no one has yet found any clue to that enigma.'

"'River Hall—where is that?' he asked; then suddenly added, 'Oh! I remember now: you mean the Uninhabited House, as it is called. Yes, there is a curious story, if you like. May I ask if you are interested in any way in that matter?'

"'Not in any way, except that I have been spending the evening there with a friend of mine.'

"'Has he seen anything of the reputed ghost?' asked my companion, eagerly. 'Is he able to throw any light on the dark subject?'

"'I don't think he can,' I replied. 'He has seen the usual appearances which I believe it is correct to see at River Hall; but so far, they have added nothing to his previous knowledge.'

"'He has seen, you say?'

"'Yes; all the orthodox lions of that cheerful house.'

"'And still he is not daunted—he is not afraid?'

"'He is not afraid. Honestly, putting ghosts entirely on one side, I should not care to be in his shoes, all alone in a lonely house.'

"'And you would be right, sir,' was the answer. 'A man must be mad to run such a risk.'

"'So I told him,' I agreed.

"'Why, I would not stay in that house alone for any money which could be offered to me,' he went on, eagerly.

"'I cannot go so far as that,' I said; 'but still it must be a very large sum which could induce me to do so.'

"'It ought to be pulled down, sir,' he continued; 'the walls ought to be razed to the ground.'

"'I suppose they will,' I answered, 'when Miss Elmsdale, the owner, comes of age; unless, indeed, our modern Don Quixote runs the ghost to earth before that time.'

119

"'Did you say the young man was ill?' asked my companion.

"'He has got a cold,' I answered.

"'And colds are nasty things to get rid of,' he commented, 'particularly in those low-lying localities. That is a most unhealthy part; you ought to order your patient a thorough change of air.'

"'I have, but he won't take advice,' was my reply. 'He has nailed his colours to the mast, and means, I believe, to stay in River Hall till he kills the ghost, or the ghost kills him.'

"'What a foolish youth!'

"'Undoubtedly; but, then, youth is generally foolish, and we have all our crotchets.'

"We had reached the other side of the bridge by this time, and saying his road lay in an opposite direction to mine, the gentleman I have sketched told me the nearest way to take, and bade me a civil good night, adding, 'I suppose I ought to say good morning.'"

"And is that all?" I asked, as Munro paused.

"Bide a wee, as the Scotch say, my son. I strode off along the road he indicated, and then, instead of making the detour he had kindly sketched out for my benefit, chose the first turning to my left, and, quite convinced he would soon pass that way, took up my position in the portico of a house which lay well in shadow. It stood a little back from the side-path, and a poor little Arab sleeping on the stone step proved to me the policeman was not over and above vigilant in that neighbourhood.

"I waited, Heaven only knows how long, thinking all the time I must be mistaken, and that his home did lie in the direction he took; but at last, looking out between the pillars and the concealing shrubs, I saw him. He was looking eagerly into the distance, with such a drawn, worn, painful expression, that for a moment my heart relented, and I thought I would let the poor devil go in peace.

"It was only for a moment, however; touching the sleeping boy, I bade him awake, if he wanted to earn a shilling. 'Keep that gentleman in sight, and get to know for me where he lives, and come back here, and I will give you a shilling, and perhaps two, for your pains.'

120

"With his eyes still heavy with slumber, and his perceptions for the moment dulled, he sped after the figure, limping wearily on. I saw him ask my late companion for charity, and follow the gentleman for a few steps, when the latter, threatening him with his stick, the boy dodged to escape a blow, and then, by way of showing how lightly his bosom's load sat upon him, began turning wheels down the middle of the street. He passed the place where I stood, and spun a hundred feet further on, then he gathered himself together, and seeing no one in sight, stealthily crept back to his porch again.

"'You young rascal,' I said, 'I told you to follow him home. I want to know his name and address particularly.'

"'Come along, then,' he answered, 'and I'll show you. Bless you, we all knows him—better than we do the police, or anybody hereabouts. He's a beak and a ward up at the church, whatever that is, and he has building-yards as big, oh! as big as two workhouses, and—'"

"His name, Munro—his name?" I gasped.

"Harringford."

I expected it. I knew then that for days and weeks my suspicions had been vaguely connecting Mr. Harringford with the mystery of the Uninhabited House.

This was the hiding figure in my dream, the link hitherto wanting in my reveries concerning River Hall. I had been looking for this—waiting for it; I understood at last; and yet, when Munro mentioned the name of the man who had thought it worth his while to watch my movements, I shrunk from the conclusion which forced itself upon me.

"Must we go on to the end with this affair?" I asked, after a pause, and my voice was so changed, it sounded like that of a stranger to me.

"We do not yet know what the end will prove," Munro answered; "but whatever it may be, we must not turn back now."

"How ought we to act, do you think?" I inquired.

"We ought not to act at all," he answered. "We had better wait and see what his next move will be. He is certain to take some step. He will try to get you out of this house by hook or by crook. He has already striven to effect his purpose through Miss Elmsdale, and failed. It will therefore be necessary for him to attempt some other scheme. It is not for me to decide on the course he is likely to pursue; but, if I were in your place, I should stay within doors at night. I should not sit in the dark near windows still unshuttered. I should not allow any strangers to enter the house, and I should have a couple of good dogs running loose about the premises. I have brought Brenda with me as a beginning, and I think I know where to lay my hand on a good old collie, who will stay near any house I am in, and let no one trespass about it with impunity."

"Good heavens! Munro, you don't mean to say you think the man would murder me!" I exclaimed.

"I don't know what he might, or might not do," he replied. "There is something about this house he is afraid may be found out, and he is afraid you will find it out. Unless I am greatly mistaken, a great deal depends upon the secret being preserved intact. At present we can only surmise its nature; but I mean, in the course of a few days, to know more of Mr. Harringford's antecedents than he might be willing to communicate to anyone. What is the matter with you, Hal? You look as white as a corpse."

"I was only thinking," I answered, "of one evening last week, when I fell asleep in the drawing-room, and woke in a fright, imagining I saw that horrid light streaming out from the library, and a face pressed up close to the glass of the window on my left hand peering into the room."

"I have no doubt the face was there," he said, gravely; "but I do not think it will come again, so long as Brenda is alive. Nevertheless, I should be careful. Desperate men are capable of desperate deeds."

The first post next morning brought me a letter from Mr. Craven, which proved Mr. Harringford entertained for the present no intention of proceeding to extremities with me.

He had been in Buckingham Street, so said my principal, and offered to buy the freehold of River Hall for twelve hundred pounds.

Mr. Craven thought he might be induced to increase his bid to fifteen hundred, and added: "Miss Blake has half consented to the arrangement, and Miss Elmsdale is eager for the matter to be pushed on, so that the transfer may take place directly she comes of age. I confess, now an actual offer has been made, I feel reluctant to sacrifice the property for such a sum, and doubt whether it might not be better to offer it for sale by auction—that is, if you think there is no chance of your discovering the reason why River Hall bears so bad a name. Have you obtained any clue to the mystery?"

To this I replied in a note, which Munro himself conveyed to the office.

"I have obtained an important clue; but that is all I can say for the present. Will you tell Mr. Harringford I am at River Hall, and that you think, being on the spot and knowing all about the place, I could negotiate the matter better than anyone else in the office? If he is desirous of purchasing, he will not object to calling some evening and discussing the matter with me. I have an idea that a large sum of money might be made out of this property by an enterprising man like Mr. Harringford; and it is just possible, after hearing what I have to say, he may find himself able to make a much better offer for the Uninhabited House than that mentioned in your note. At all events, the interview can do no harm. I am still suffering so much from cold that it would be imprudent for me to wait upon Mr. Harringford, which would otherwise be only courteous on my part."

"Capital!" said Munro, reading over my shoulder. "That will bring my gentleman to River Hall—. But what is wrong, Patterson? You are surely not going to turn chickenhearted now?"

"No," I answered; "but I wish it was over. I dread something, and I do not know what it is. Though nothing shall induce me to waver, I am afraid, Munro. I am not ashamed to say it: I am afraid, as I was the first night I stayed in this house. I am not a coward, but I am afraid."

He did not reply for a moment. He walked to the window and looked out over the Thames; then he came back, and, wringing my hand, said, in tones that tried unsuccessfully to be cheerful:

"I know what it is, old fellow. Do you think I have not had the feeling myself, since I came here? But remember, it has to be done, and I will stand by you. I will see you through it."

"It won't do for you to be in the room, though," I suggested.

"No; but I will stay within earshot," he answered.

123

We did not talk much more about the matter. Men rarely do talk much about anything which seems to them very serious, and I may candidly say that I had never felt anything in my life to be much more serious than that impending interview with Mr. Harringford.

That he would come we never doubted for a moment, and we were right. As soon as it was possible for him to appoint an interview, Mr. Harringford did so.

"Nine o'clock on to-morrow (Thursday) evening," was the hour he named, apologizing at the same time for being unable to call at an earlier period of the day.

"Humph!" said Munro, turning the note over. "You will receive him in the library, of course, Hal?"

I replied such was my intention.

"And that will be a move for which he is in no way prepared," commented my friend.

From the night when Munro walked and talked with Mr. Harringford, no person came spying round and about the Uninhabited House. Of this fact we were satisfied, for Brenda, who gave tongue at the slightest murmur wafted over the river from the barges lying waiting for the tide, never barked as though she were on the track of living being; whilst the collie—a tawny-black, unkempt, ill-conditioned, savage-natured, but yet most true and faithful brute, which Munro insisted on keeping within doors, never raised his voice from the day he arrived at River Hall, till the night Mr. Harringford rang the visitor's-bell, when the animal, who had been sleeping with his nose resting on his paws, lifted his head and indulged in a prolonged howl.

Not a nice beginning to an interview which I dreaded.

A TERRIBLE INTERVIEW

I was in the library, waiting to receive Mr. Harringford. A bright fire blazed on the hearth, the table was strewn with papers Munro had brought to me from the office, the gas was all ablaze, and the room looked bright and cheerful—as bright and as cheerful as if no ghost had been ever heard of in connection with it.

At a few minutes past nine my visitor arrived. Mrs. Stott ushered him into the library, and he entered the room evidently intending to shake hands with me, which civility I affected not to notice.

After the first words of greeting were exchanged, I asked if he would have tea, or coffee, or wine; and finding he rejected all offers of refreshment, I rang the bell and told Mrs. Stott I could dispense with her attendance for the night.

"Do you mean to tell me you stay in this house entirely alone?" asked my visitor.

"Until Mrs. Stott came I was quite alone," I answered.

"I would not have done it for any consideration," he remarked.

"Possibly not," I replied. "People are differently constituted."

It was not long before we got to business. His offer of twelve hundred pounds I pooh-poohed as ridiculous.

"Well," he said—by this time I knew I had a keen man of business to deal with—"put the place up to auction, and see whether you will get as much."

"There are two, or rather, three ways of dealing with the property, which have occurred to me, Mr. Harringford," I explained. "One is letting or selling this house for a reformatory, or school. Ghosts in that case won't trouble the inmates, we may be quite certain; another is utilizing the buildings for a manufactory; and the third is laying the ground out for building purposes, thus—"

As I spoke, I laid before him a plan for a tri-sided square of building, the south side being formed by the river. I had taken great pains with the drawing of this plan: the future houses, the future square, the future riverwalk with seats at intervals, were all to be found in the roll which I unfolded and laid before him, and the effect my sketch produced surprised me.

"In Heaven's name, Mr. Patterson," he asked, "where did you get this? You never drew it out of your own head!"

I hastened to assure him I had certainly not got it out of any other person's head; but he smiled incredulously.

"Probably," he suggested, "Mr. Elmsdale left some such sketch behind him—something, at all events, which suggested the idea to you."

"If he did, I never saw nor heard of it," I answered.

"You may have forgotten the circumstance," he persisted; "but I feel confident you must have seen something like this before. Perhaps amongst the papers in Mr. Craven's office."

"May I inquire why you have formed such an opinion?" I said, a little stiffly.

"Simply because this tri-sided square was a favourite project of the late owner of River Hall," he replied. "After the death of his wife, the place grew distasteful to him, and I have often heard him say he would convert the ground into one of the handsomest squares in the neighbourhood of London. All he wanted was a piece of additional land lying to the west, which piece is, I believe, now to be had at a price—"

I sat like one stricken dumb. By no mental process, for which I could ever account, had that idea been evolved. It sprang into life at a bound. It came to me in my sleep, and I wakened at once with the whole plan clear and distinct before my mind's eye, as it now lay clear and distinct before Mr. Harringford.

"It is very extraordinary," I managed at last to stammer out; "for I can honestly say I never heard even a suggestion of Mr. Elmsdale's design; indeed, I did not know he had ever thought of building upon the ground."

"Such was the fact, however," replied my visitor. "He was a speculative man in many ways. Yes, very speculative, and full of plans and projects. However, Mr. Patterson," he proceeded, "all this only proves the truth of the old remark, that 'great wits and little wits sometimes jump together.'"

126

There was a ring of sarcasm in his voice, as in his words, but I did not give much heed to it. The design, then, was not mine. It had come to me in sleep, it had been forced upon me, it had been explained to me in a word, and as I asked myself, By whom? I was unable to repress a shudder.

"You are not well, I fear," said Mr. Harringford; "this place seems to have affected your health. Surely you have acted imprudently in risking so much to gain so little."

"I do not agree with you," I replied. "However, time will show whether I have been right or wrong in coming here. I have learned many things of which I was previously in ignorance, and I think I hold a clue in my hands which, properly followed, may lead me to the hidden mystery of River Hall."

"Indeed!" he exclaimed. "May I ask the nature of that clue?"

"It would be premature for me to say more than this, that I am inclined to doubt whether Mr. Elmsdale committed suicide."

"Do you think his death was the result of accident, then?" he inquired, his face blanching to a ghastly whiteness.

"No, I do not," I answered, bluntly. "But my thoughts can have little interest for anyone, at present. What we want to talk about is the sale and purchase of this place. The offer you made to Mr. Craven, I consider ridiculous. Let on building lease, the land alone would bring in a handsome income, and the house ought to sell for about as much as you offer for the whole property."

"Perhaps it might, if you could find a purchaser," he answered; "and the land might return an income, if you could let it as you suggest; but, in the meantime, while the grass grows, the steed starves; and while you are waiting for your buyer and your speculative builder, Miss Blake and Miss Elmsdale will have to walk barefoot, waiting for shoes you may never be able to provide for them."

There was truth in this, but only a half-truth, I felt, so I said:

"When examined at the inquest, Mr. Harringford, you stated, I think, that you were under considerable obligations to Mr. Elmsdale?"

"Did I?" he remarked. "Possibly, he had given me a helping-hand once

127

or twice, and probably I mentioned the fact. It is a long time ago, though."

"Not so very long," I answered; "not long enough, I should imagine, to enable you to forget any benefits you may have received from Mr. Elmsdale."

"Mr. Patterson," he interrupted, "are we talking business or sentiment? If the former, please understand I have my own interests to attend to, and that I mean to attend to them. If the latter, I am willing, if you say Miss Elmsdale has pressing need for the money, to send her my cheque for fifty or a hundred pounds. Charity is one thing, trade another, and I do not care to mix them. I should never have attained to my present position, had I allowed fine feelings to interfere with the driving of a bargain. I don't want River Hall. I would not give that," and he snapped his fingers, "to have the title-deeds in my hands to-morrow; but as Miss Elmsdale wishes to sell, and as no one else will buy, I offer what I consider a fair price for the place. If you think you can do better, well and good. If—"

He stopped suddenly in his sentence, then rising, he cried, "It is a trick—a vile, infamous, disgraceful trick!" while his utterance grew thick, and his face began to work like that of a person in convulsions.

"What do you mean?" I asked, rising also, and turning to look in the direction he indicated with outstretched arm and dilated eyes.

Then I saw—no need for him to answer. Standing in the entrance to the strong room was Robert Elmsdale himself, darkness for a background, the light of the gas falling full upon his face.

Slowly, sternly, he came forward, step by step. With footfalls that fell noiselessly, he advanced across the carpet, moving steadily forward towards Mr. Harringford, who, beating the air with his hands, screamed, "Keep him off! don't let him touch me!" and fell full length on the floor.

Next instant, Munro was in the room. "Hullo, what is the matter?" he asked. "What have you done to him—what has he been doing to you?"

I could not answer. Looking in my face, I think Munro understood we had both seen that which no man can behold unappalled.

"Come, Hal," he said, "bestir yourself. Whatever has happened, don't sink under it like a woman. Help me to lift him. Merciful Heaven!" he

128

added, as he raised the prostrate figure. "He is dead!"

To this hour, I do not know how we managed to carry him into the drawing-room. I cannot imagine how our trembling hands bore that inert body out of the library and across the hall. It seems like a dream to me calling up Mrs. Stott, and then tearing away from the house in quest of further medical help, haunted, every step I took, by the memory of that awful presence, the mere sight of which had stricken down one of us in the midst of his buying, and bargaining, and boasting.

I had done it—I had raised that ghost—I had brought the man to his death; and as I fled through the night, innocent as I had been of the thought of such a catastrophe, I understood what Cain must have felt when he went out to live his life with the brand of murderer upon him.

But the man was not dead; though he lay for hours like one from whom life had departed, he did not die then. We had all the genius, and knowledge, and skill of London at his service. If doctors could have saved him, he had lived. If nursing could have availed him, he had recovered, for I never left him.

When the end came I was almost worn out myself.

And the end came very soon.

"No more doctors," whispered the sick man; "they cannot cure me. Send for a clergyman, and a lawyer, Mr. Craven as well as any other. It is all over now; and better so; life is but a long fever. Perhaps he will sleep now, and let me sleep too. Yes, I killed him. Why, I will tell you. Give me some wine.

"What I said at the inquest about owing my worldly prosperity to him was true. I trace my pecuniary success to Mr. Elmsdale; but I trace also hours, months, and years of anguish to his agency. My God! the nights that man has made me spend when he was living, the nights I have spent in consequence of his death—"

He stopped; he had mentally gone back over a long journey. He was retracing the road he had travelled, from youth to old age. For he was old, if not in years, in sorrow. Lying on his death-bed, he understood for what a game he had burnt his candle to the socket; comprehended how the agony,

129

and the suspense, and the suffering, and the long, long fever of life, which with him never knew a remittent moment, had robbed him of that which every man has a right to expect, some pleasure in the course of his existence.

"When I first met Elmsdale," he went on, "I was a young man, and an ambitious one. I was a clerk in the City. I had been married a couple of years to a wife I loved dearly. She was possessed of only a small dot; and after furnishing our house, and paying for all the expenses incident on the coming of a first child, we thought ourselves fortunate in knowing there was still a deposit standing in our name at the Joint-Stock Bank, for something over two hundred pounds.

"Nevertheless, I was anxious. So far, we had lived within our income; but with an annual advance of salary only amounting to ten pounds, or thereabouts, I did not see how we were to manage when more children came, particularly as the cost of living increased day by day. It was a dear year that of which I am speaking.

"I do not precisely remember on what occasion it was I first saw Mr. Elmsdale; but I knew afterwards he picked me out as a person likely to be useful to him.

"He was on good terms with my employers, and asked them to allow me to bid for some houses he wanted to purchase at a sale.

"To this hour I do not know why he did not bid for them himself. He gave me a five-pound note for my services; and that was the beginning of our connection. Off and on, I did many things for him of one sort or another, and made rather a nice addition to my salary out of doing them, till the devil, or he, or both, put it into my head to start as builder and speculator on my own account.

"I had two hundred pounds and my furniture: that was the whole of my capital; but Elmsdale found me money. I thought my fortune was made, the day he advanced me my first five hundred pounds. If I had known—if I had known—"

"Don't talk any more," I entreated. "What can it avail to speak of such matters now?"

He turned towards me impatiently.

"Not talk," he repeated, "when I have for years been as one dumb, and at length the string of my tongue is loosened! Not talk, when, if I keep silence now, he will haunt me in eternity, as he has haunted me in time!"

I did not answer, I only moistened his parched lips, and bathed his burning forehead as tenderly as my unaccustomed hands understood how to perform such offices.

"Lift me up a little, please," he said; and I put the pillows in position as deftly as I could.

"You are not a bad fellow," he remarked, "but I am not going to leave you anything."

"God forbid!" I exclaimed, involuntarily.

"Are not you in want of money?" he asked.

"Not of yours," I answered.

"Mine," he said; "it is not mine, it is his. He thought a great deal of money, and he has come back for it. He can't rest, and he won't let me rest till I have paid him principal and interest—compound interest. Yes—well, I am able to do even that."

We sat silent for a few minutes, then he spoke again.

"When I first went into business with my borrowed capital, nothing I touched really succeeded. I found myself going back—back. Far better was my position as clerk; then at least I slept sound at nights, and relished my meals. But I had tasted of so-called independence, and I could not go back to be at the beck and call of an employer. Ah! no employer ever made me work so hard as Mr. Elmsdale; no beck and call were ever so imperative as his.

"I pass over a long time of anxiety, struggle, and hardship. The world thought me a prosperous man; probably no human being, save Mr. Elmsdale, understood my real position, and he made my position almost unendurable.

"How I came first to bet on races, would be a long story, longer than I have time to tell; but my betting began upon a very small scale, and I always won—always in the beginning. I won so certainly and so continuously, that finally I began to hope for deliverance from Mr. Elmsdale's clutches.

131

"I don't know how"—the narrative was not recited straight on as I am writing it, but by starts, as strength served him—"Mr. Elmsdale ascertained I was devoting myself to the turf: all I can say is, he did ascertain the fact, and followed me down to Ascot to make sure there was no mistake in his information.

"At the previous Derby my luck had begun to turn. I had lost then—lost heavily for me, and he taxed me with having done so.

"In equity, and at law, he had then the power of foreclosing on every house and rood of ground I owned. I was in his power—in the power of Robert Elmsdale. Think of it—. But you never knew him. Young man, you ought to kneel down and thank God you were never so placed as to be in the power of such a devil—

"If ever you should get into the power of a man like Robert Elmsdale, don't offend him. It is bad enough to owe him money; but it is worse for him to owe you a grudge. I had offended him. He was always worrying me about his wife—lamenting her ill-health, extolling her beauty, glorifying himself on having married a woman of birth and breeding; just as if his were the only wife in the world, as if other men had not at home women twice as good, if not as handsome as Miss Blake's sister.

"Under Miss Blake's insolence I had writhed; and once, when my usual prudence deserted me, I told Mr. Elmsdale I had been in Ireland and seen the paternal Blake's ancestral cabin, and ascertained none of the family had ever mixed amongst the upper thousand, or whatever the number may be which goes to make up society in the Isle of Saints.

"It was foolish, and it was wrong; but I could not help saying what I did, and from that hour he was my enemy. Hitherto, he had merely been my creditor. My own imprudent speech transformed him into a man lying in wait to ruin me.

"He bided his time. He was a man who could wait for years before he struck, but who would never strike till he could make sure of inflicting a mortal wound. He drew me into his power more and more, and then he told me he did not intend to continue trusting anyone who betted—that he must have his money. If he had not it by a certain date, which he named, he would foreclose.

"That meant he would beggar me, and I with an ailing wife and a large family!

"I appealed to him. I don't remember now what I said, but I do recollect I might as well have talked to stone.

"What I endured during the time which followed, I could not describe, were I to talk for ever. Till a man in extremity tries to raise money, he never understands the difficulty of doing so. I had been short of money every hour since I first engaged in business, and yet I never comprehended the meaning of a dead-lock till then.

"One day, in the City, when I was almost mad with anxiety, I met Mr. Elmsdale.

"'Shall you be ready for me, Harringford?' he asked.

"'I do not know—I hope so,' I answered.

"'Well, remember, if you are not prepared with the money, I shall be prepared to act,' he said, with an evil smile.

"As I walked home that evening, an idea flashed into my mind. I had tried all honest means of raising the money; I would try dishonest. My credit was good. I had large transactions with first-rate houses. I was in the habit of discounting largely, and I—well, I signed names to paper that I ought not to have done. I had the bills put through. I had four months and three days in which to turn round, and I might, by that time, be able to raise sufficient to retire the acceptances.

"In the meantime, I could face Mr. Elmsdale, and so I wrote, appointing an evening when I would call with the money, and take his release for all claims upon me.

"When I arrived at River Hall he had all the necessary documents ready, but refused to give them up in exchange for my cheque.

"He could not trust me, he said, and he had, moreover, no banking account. If I liked to bring the amount in notes, well and good; if not, he would instruct his solicitors.

"The next day I had important business to attend to, so a stormy interview ended in my writing 'pay cash' on the cheque, and his consenting to take it to my bankers himself.

"My business on the following day, which happened to be out of town, detained me much longer than I anticipated, and it was late before I could reach River Hall. Late though it was, however, I determined to go after my papers. I held Mr. Elmsdale's receipt for the cheque, certainly; but I knew I had not an hour to lose in putting matters in train for another loan, if I was to retire the forged acceptances. By experience, I knew how the months slipped away when money had to be provided at the end of them, and I was feverishly anxious to hold my leases and title-deeds once more.

"I arrived at the door leading to the library. Mr. Elmsdale opened it as wide as the chain would permit, and asked who was there. I told him, and, grumbling a little at the unconscionable hour at which I had elected to pay my visit, he admitted me.

"He was out of temper. He had hoped and expected, I knew, to find payment of the cheque refused, and he could not submit with equanimity to seeing me slip out of his hands.

"Evidently, he did not expect me to come that night, for his table was strewed with deeds and notes, which he had been reckoning up, no doubt, as a miser counts his gold.

"A pair of pistols lay beside his desk—close to my hand, as I took the seat he indicated.

"We talked long and bitterly. It does not matter now what he said or I said. We fenced round and about a quarrel during the whole interview. I was meek, because I wanted him to let me have part of the money at all events on loan again; and he was blatant and insolent because he fancied I cringed to him—and I did cringe.

"I prayed for help that night from Man as I have never since prayed for help from God.

"You are still young, Mr. Patterson, and life, as yet, is new to you, or else I would ask whether, in going into an entirely strange office, you have not, if agitated in mind, picked up from the table a letter or card, and kept twisting it about, utterly unconscious for the time being of the social solecism you were committing.

"In precisely the same spirit—God is my witness, as I am a dying man, with no object to serve in speaking falsehoods—while we talked, I took up one of the pistols and commenced handling it.

"'Take care,' he said; 'that is loaded'; hearing which I laid it down again.

"For a time we went on talking; he trying to ascertain how I had obtained the money, I striving to mislead him.

"'Come, Mr. Elmsdale,' I remarked at last, 'you see I have been able to raise the money; now be friendly, and consent to advance me a few thousands, at a fair rate, on a property I am negotiating for. There is no occasion, surely, for us to quarrel, after all the years we have done business together. Say you will give me a helping-hand once more, and—'

"Then he interrupted me, and swore, with a great oath, he would never have another transaction with me.

"'Though you have paid me,' he said, 'I know you are hopelessly insolvent. I cannot tell where or how you have managed to raise that money, but certain am I it has been by deceiving some one; and so sure as I stand here I will know all about the transaction within a month.'

"While we talked, he had been, at intervals, passing to and from his strong room, putting away the notes and papers previously lying about on the table; and, as he made this last observation, he was standing just within the door, placing something on the shelf.

"'It is of no use talking to me any more,' he went on. 'If you talked from now to eternity you could not alter my decision. There are your deeds; take them, and never let me see you in my house again.'

"He came out of the darkness into the light at that moment, looking burly, and insolent, and braggart, as was his wont.

"Something in his face, in the tone of his voice, in the vulgar assumption of his manner, maddened me. I do not know, I have never been able to tell, what made me long at that moment to kill him—but I did long. With an impulse I could not resist, I rose as he returned towards the table, and snatching a pistol from the table—fired.

"Before he could realize my intention, the bullet was in his brain. He was dead, and I a murderer.

135

"You can understand pretty well what followed. I ran into the passage and opened the door; then, finding no one seemed to have heard the report of the pistol, my senses came back to me. I was not sorry for what I had done. All I cared for was to avert suspicion from myself, and to secure some advantage from his death.

"Stealing back into the room, I took all the money I could find, as well as deeds and other securities. These last I destroyed next day, and in doing so I felt a savage satisfaction.

"He would have served them the same as me,' I thought. All the rest you know pretty well.

"From the hour I left him lying dead in the library every worldly plan prospered with me. If I invested in land, it trebled in value. Did I speculate in houses, they were sought after as investments. I grew rich, respected, a man of standing. I had sold my soul to the devil, and he paid me even higher wages than those for which I engaged—but there was a balance.

"One after another, wife and children died; and while my heart was breaking by reason of my home left desolate, there came to me the first rumour of this place being haunted.

"I would not believe it—I did not—I fought against the truth as men fight with despair.

"I used to come here at night and wander as near to the house as I safely could. The place dogged me, sleeping and waking. That library was an ever-present memory. I have sat in my lonely rooms till I could endure the horrors of imagination no longer, and been forced to come from London that I might look at this terrible house, with the silent river flowing sullenly past its desolate gardens.

"Life seemed ebbing away from me. I saw that day by day the blood left my cheeks. I looked at my hands, and beheld they were becoming like those of some one very aged. My lameness grew perceptible to others as well as to me, and I could distinguish, as I walked in the sunshine, the shadow my figure threw was that of one deformed. I grew weak, and worn, and tired, yet I never thoroughly lost heart till I knew you had come here to unravel the secret.

136

"'And it will be revealed to him,' I thought, 'if I do not kill him too.'

"You have been within an ace of death often and often since you set yourself this task, but at the last instant my heart always failed me.

"Well, you are to live, and I to die. It was to be so, I suppose; but you will never be nearer your last moment, till you lie a corpse, than you have been twice, at any rate."

Then I understood how accurately Munro had judged when he warned me to be on my guard against this man—now harmless and dying, but so recently desperate and all-powerful for evil; and as I recalled the nights I had spent in that desolate house, I shivered.

Even now, though the years have come and the years have gone since I kept my lonely watch in River Hall, I start sometimes from sleep with a great horror of darkness upon me, and a feeling that stealthily some one is creeping through the silence to take my life!

CONCLUSION

I can remember the day and the hour as if it had all happened yesterday. I can recall the view from the windows distinctly, as though time had stood still ever since. There are no gardens under our windows in Buckingham Street. Buckingham Gate stands the entrance to a desert of mud, on which the young Arabs—shoeless, stockingless—are disporting themselves. It is low water, and the river steamers keep towards the middle arches of Waterloo. Up aloft the Hungerford Suspension rears itself in mid air, and that spick-and-span new bridge, across which trains run now ceaselessly, has not yet been projected. It is a bright spring day. The sunshine falls upon the buildings on the Surrey side, and lights them with a picturesque beauty to which they have not the slightest title. A barge, laden with hay, is lying almost motionless in the middle of the Thames.

There is, even in London, a great promise and hope about that pleasant spring day, but for me life has held no promise, and the future no hope, since that night when the mystery of River Hall was solved in my presence, and out of his own mouth the murderer uttered his condemnation.

How the weeks and the months had passed with me is soon told. Ill when I left River Hall, shortly after my return home I fell sick unto death, and lay like one who had already entered the Valley of the Shadow.

I was too weak to move; I was too faint to think; and when at length I was brought slowly back to the recollection of life and its cares, of all I had experienced and suffered in the Uninhabited House, the time spent in it seemed to me like the memory of some frightful dream.

I had lost my health there, and my love too. Helena was now further removed from me than ever. She was a great heiress. Mr. Harringford had left her all his money absolutely, and already Miss Blake was considering which of the suitors, who now came rushing to woo, it would be best for her niece to wed.

As for me, Taylor repeated, by way of a good joke, that her aunt referred to me as a "decent sort of young man" who "seemed to be but weakly," and, ignoring the fact of ever having stated "she would not mind giving fifty pounds," remarked to Mr. Craven, that, if I was in poor circumstances, he might pay me five or ten sovereigns, and charge the amount to her account.

Of all this Mr. Craven said nothing to me. He only came perpetually to my sick-bed, and told my mother that whenever I was able to leave town I must get away, drawing upon him for whatever sums I might require. I did not need to encroach on his kindness, however, for my uncle, hearing of my illness, sent me a cordial invitation to spend some time with him.

In his cottage, far away from London, strength at last returned to me, and by the autumn my old place in Mr. Craven's office was no longer vacant. I sat in my accustomed corner, pursuing former avocations, a changed man.

I was hard-working as ever, but hope lightened my road no longer.

To a penny I knew the amount of my lady's fortune, and understood Mr. Harringford's bequest had set her as far above me as the stars are above the earth.

I had the conduct of most of Miss Elmsdale's business. As a compliment, perhaps, Mr. Craven entrusted all the work connected with Mr. Harringford's estate to me, and I accepted that trust as I should have done any other which he might choose to place in my hands.

But I could have dispensed with his well-meant kindness. Every visit I paid to Miss Blake filled my soul with bitterness. Had I been a porter, a crossing-sweeper, or a potman, she might, I suppose, have treated me with some sort of courtesy; but, as matters stood, her every tone, word, and look, said, plainly as possible, "If you do not know your station, I will teach it to you."

As for Helena, she was always the same—sweet, and kind, and grateful, and gracious; but she had her friends about her: new lovers waiting for her smiles. And, after a time, the shadow cast across her youth would, I understood, be altogether removed, and leave her free to begin a new and beautiful life, unalloyed by that hideous, haunting memory of suicide, which had changed into melancholy the gay cheerfulness of her lovely girlhood.

Yes; it was the old story of the streamlet and the snow, of the rose and the wind. To others my love might not have seemed hopeless, but to me it was dead as the flowers I had seen blooming a year before.

Not for any earthly consideration would I have made a claim upon her affection.

What I had done had been done freely and loyally. I gave it all to her as utterly as I had previously given my heart, and now I could make no bargain with my dear. I never for a moment thought she owed me anything for my pains and trouble. Her kindly glances, her sweet words, her little, thoughtful turns of manner, were free gifts of her goodness, but in no sense payment for my services.

She understood I could not presume upon them, and was, perhaps, better satisfied it should be so.

But nothing satisfied Miss Blake, and at length between her and Mr. Craven there ensued a serious disagreement. She insisted he should not "send that clerk of his" to the house again, and suggested if Mr. Craven were too high and mighty to attend to the concerns of Miss Elmsdale himself, Miss Blake must look out for another solicitor.

"The sooner the better, madam," said Mr. Craven, with great state; and Miss Blake left in a huff, and actually did go off to a rival attorney, who, however, firmly declined to undertake her business.

Then Helena came as peacemaker. She smoothed down Mr. Craven's ruffled feathers and talked him into a good temper, and effected a reconciliation with her aunt, and then nearly spoilt everything by adding:

"But indeed I think Mr. Patterson had better not come to see us for the present, at all events."

"You ungrateful girl!" exclaimed Mr. Craven; but she answered, with a little sob, that she was not ungrateful, only—only she thought it would be better if I stayed away.

And so Taylor took my duties on him, and, as a natural consequence, some very pretty disputes between him and Miss Blake had to be arranged by Mr. Craven.

Thus the winter passed, and it was spring again—that spring day of which I have spoken. Mr. Craven and I were alone in the office. He had come late into town and was reading his letters; whilst I, seated by a

140

window overlooking the Thames, gave about equal attention to the river outside and a tedious document lying on my table.

We had not spoken a word, I think, for ten minutes, when a slip of paper was brought in, on which was written a name.

"Ask her to walk in," said Mr. Craven, and, going to the door, he greeted the visitor, and led Miss Elmsdale into the room.

I rose, irresolute; but she came forward, and, with a charming blush, held out her hand, and asked me some commonplace question about my health.

Then I was going, but she entreated me not to leave the room on her account.

"This is my birthday, Mr. Craven," she went on, "and I have come to ask you to wish me many happy returns of the day, and to do something for me—will you?"

"I wish you every happiness, my dear," he answered, with a tenderness born, perhaps, of olden memories and of loving-kindness towards one so sweet, and beautiful, and lonely. "And if there is anything I can do for you on your birthday, why, it is done, that is all I can say."

She clasped her dear hands round his arm, and led him towards a further window. I could see her downcast eyes—the long lashes lying on her cheeks, the soft colour flitting and coming, making her alternately pale and rosy, and I was jealous. Heaven forgive me! If she had hung so trustfully about one of the patriarchs, I should have been jealous, though he reckoned his years by centuries.

What she had to say was said quickly. She spoke in a whisper, bringing her lips close to his ear, and lifting her eyes imploringly to his when she had finished.

"Upon my word, miss," he exclaimed, aloud, and he held her from him and looked at her till the colour rushed in beautiful blushes even to her temples, and her lashes were wet with tears, and her cheeks dimpled with smiles. "Upon my word—and you make such a request to me—to me, who have a character to maintain, and who have daughters of my own to whom I am bound to set a good example! Patterson, come here. Can you imagine

141

what this young lady wants me to do for her now? She is twenty-one to-day, she tells me, and she wants me to ask you to marry her. She says she will never marry anyone else." Then, as I hung back a little, dazed, fearful, and unable to credit the evidence of my senses, he added:

"Take her; she means it every word, and you deserve to have her. If she had chosen anybody else I would never have drawn out her settlements."

But I would not take her, not then. Standing there with the spring landscape blurred for the moment before me, I tried to tell them both what I felt. At first, my words were low and broken, for the change from misery to happiness affected me almost as though I had been suddenly plunged from happiness into despair. But by degrees I recovered my senses, and told my darling and Mr. Craven it was not fit she should, out of very generosity, give herself to me—a man utterly destitute of fortune—a man who, though he loved her better than life, was only a clerk at a clerk's salary.

"If I were a duke," I went on, breaking ground at last, "with a duke's revenue and a duke's rank, I should only value what I had for her sake. I would carry my money, and my birth, and my position to her, and ask her to take all, if she would only take me with them; but, as matters stand, Mr. Craven—"

"I owe everything worth having in life to you," she said, impetuously, taking my hand in hers. "I should not like you at all if you were a duke, and had a ducal revenue."

"I think you are too strait-laced, Patterson," agreed Mr. Craven. "She does owe everything she has to your determination, remember."

"But I undertook to solve the mystery for fifty pounds," I remarked, smiling in spite of myself.

"Which has never been paid," remarked my employer. "But," he went on, "you young people come here and sit down, and let us talk the affair over all together." And so he put us in chairs as if we had been clients, while he took his professional seat, and, after a pause, began:

"My dear Helena, I think the young man has reason. A woman should marry her equal. He will, in a worldly sense, be more than your equal some day; but that is nothing. A man should be head of the household.

142

"It is good, and nice, and loving of you, my child, to wish to endow your husband with all your worldly goods; but your husband ought, before he takes you, to have goods of his own wherewith to endow you. Now, now, now, don't purse up your pretty mouth, and try to controvert a lawyer's wisdom. You are both young: you have plenty of time before you.

"He ought to be given an opportunity of showing what he can do, and you ought to mix in society and see whether you meet anyone you think you can like better. There is no worse time for finding out a mistake of that sort, than after marriage." And so the kind soul prosed on, and would, possibly, have gone on prosing for a few hours more, had I not interrupted one of his sentences by saying I would not have Miss Elmsdale bound by any engagement, or consider herself other than free as air.

"Well, well," he answered, testily, "we understand that thoroughly. But I suppose you do not intend to cast the young lady's affections from you as if they were of no value?"

At this juncture her eyes and mine met. She smiled, and I could not help smiling too.

"Suppose we leave it in this way," Mr. Craven said, addressing apparently some independent stranger. "If, at the end of a year, Miss Elmsdale is of the same mind, let her write to me and say so. That course will leave her free enough, and it will give us twelve months in which to turn round, and see what we can do in the way of making his fortune. I do not imagine he will ever be able to count down guineas against her guineas, or that he wants to do anything so absurd. But he is right in saying an heiress should not marry a struggling clerk. He ought to be earning a good income before he is much older, and he shall, or my name is not William Craven."

I got up and shook his hand, and Helena kissed him.

"Tut, tut! fie, fie! what's all this?" he exclaimed, searching sedulously for his double eyeglass—which all the while he held between his finger and thumb. "Now, young people, you must not occupy my time any longer. Harry, see this self-willed little lady into a cab; and you need not return until the afternoon. If you are in time to find me before I leave, that will do quite

143

well. Good-bye, Miss Helena."

I did not take his hint, though. Failing to find a cab—perhaps for want of looking for one—I ventured to walk with my beautiful companion up Regent Street as far as Oxford Circus.

Through what enchanted ground we passed in that short distance, how can I ever hope to tell! It was all like a story of fairyland, with Helena for Queen of Unreality. But it was real enough. Ah! my dear, you knew your own mind, as I, after years and years of wedded happiness, can testify.

Next day, Mr. Craven started off to the west of England. He did not tell me where he was going; indeed, I never knew he had been to see my uncle until long afterwards.

What he told that gentleman, what he said of me and Helena, of my poor talents and her beauty, may be gathered from the fact that the old admiral agreed first to buy me a partnership in some established firm, and then swore a mighty oath, that if the heiress was, at the end of twelve months, willing to marry his nephew, he would make him his heir.

"I should like to have you with me, Patterson," said Mr. Craven, when we were discussing my uncle's proposal, which a few weeks after took me greatly by surprise; "but, if you remain here, Miss Blake will always regard you as a clerk. I know of a good opening; trust me to arrange everything satisfactorily for you."

Whether Miss Blake, even with my altered fortunes, would ever have become reconciled to the match, is extremely doubtful, had the beau monde not turned a very decided cold-shoulder to the Irish patriot.

Helena, of course, everyone wanted, but Miss Blake no one wanted; and the fact was made very patent to that lady.

"They'll be for parting you and me, my dear," said the poor creature one day, when society had proved more than usually cruel. "If ever I am let see you after your marriage, I suppose I shall have to creep in at the area-door, and make believe I am some faithful old nurse wanting to have a look at my dear child's sweet face."

"No one shall ever separate me from you, dear, silly aunt," said my charmer, kissing first one of her relative's high cheek-bones, and then the other.

"We'll have to jog on, two old spinsters together, then, I am thinking," replied Miss Blake.

"No," was the answer, very distinctly spoken. "I am going to marry Mr. Henry Patterson, and he will not ask me to part from my ridiculous, foolish aunt."

"Patterson! that conceited clerk of William Craven's? Why, he has not darkened our doors for fifteen months and more."

"Quite true," agreed her niece; "but, nevertheless, I am going to marry him. I asked him to marry me a year ago."

"You don't mane that, Helena!" said poor Miss Blake. "You should not talk like an infant in arms."

"We are only waiting for your consent," went on my lady fair.

"Then that you will never have. While I retain my powers of speech you shall not marry a pauper who has only asked you for the sake of your money."

"He did not ask me; I asked him," said Helena, mischievously; "and he is not a beggar. His uncle has bought him a partnership, and is going to leave him his money; and he will be here himself to-morrow, to tell you all about his prospects."

At first, Miss Blake refused to see me; but after a time she relented, and, thankful, perhaps, to have once again anyone over whom she could tyrannise, treated her niece's future husband—as Helena declared—most shamefully.

"But you two must learn to agree, for there shall be no quarrelling in our house," added the pretty autocrat.

"You needn't trouble yourself about that, Helena," said her aunt.

"He'll be just like all the rest. If he's civil to me before marriage, he won't be after. He will soon find out there is no place in the house, or, for that matter, in the world, for Susan Blake"; and my enemy, for the first time in my memory, fairly broke down and began to whimper.

"Miss Blake," I said, "how can I convince you that I never dreamt, never could dream of asking you and Helena to separate?"

"See that, now, and he calls you Helena already," said the lady, reproachfully.

"Well, he must begin sometime. And that reminds me the sooner he begins to call you aunt, the better."

I did not begin to do so then, of that the reader may be quite certain; but there came a day when the word fell quite naturally from my lips.

For a long period ours was a hollow truce, but, as time passed on, and I resolutely refused to quarrel with Miss Blake, she gradually ceased trying to pick quarrels with me.

Our home is very dear to her. All the household management Helena from the first hour took into her own hands; but in the nursery Miss Blake reigns supreme.

She has always a grievance, but she is thoroughly happy. She dresses now like other people, and wears over her gray hair caps of Helena's selection.

Time has softened some of her prejudices, and age renders her eccentricities less noticeable; but she is still, after her fashion, unique, and we feel in our home, as we used to feel in the office—that we could better spare a better man.

The old house was pulled down, and not a square, but a fine terrace occupied its site. Munro lives in one of those desirable tenements, and is growing rich and famous day by day. Mr. Craven has retired from practice, and taken a place in the country, where he is bored to death though he professes himself charmed with the quiet.

Helena and I have always been town-dwellers. Though the Uninhabited House is never mentioned by either of us, she knows I have still a shuddering horror of lonely places.

My experiences in the Uninhabited House have made me somewhat nervous. Why, it was only the other night—

"What are you doing, making all that spluttering on your paper?" says an interrupting voice at this juncture, and, looking up, I see Miss Blake seated by the window, clothed and in her right mind.

"You had better put by that writing," she proceeds, with the manner of

146

one having authority, and I am so amazed, when I contrast Miss Blake as she is, with what she was, that I at once obey!

THE END

Made in United States
Orlando, FL
10 October 2023

37748424R10080